turbo

PROLOG
FOREWORD

»Exclusive. Explosive. Expensive.« Dieser Werbe-slogan aus den siebziger Jahren bringt die Eigen-schaften des Porsche 911 Turbo treffend auf den Punkt. Seit über 30 Jahren gilt er als Automobil-Ikone und als der Sportwagen schlechthin. Seine einmalige Kombination aus Leistung und Luxus haben den 911 Turbo zu einem Klassiker reifen lassen, der in der Porsche-Geschichte einen besonderen Platz einnimmt.

Wie in keinem anderen Modell spiegelt sich in den inzwischen sieben Turbo-Generationen die Innovations-kraft der Marke Porsche wider. Als Technologieträger führte er zahlreiche technische Neuerungen in den Automobilbau ein. Dabei blieb er nicht nur dem Leis-tungsgedanken treu, sondern entsprach auch stets dem Wunsch von Ferry Porsche nach hoher Motorleis-tung bei geringem Verbrauch.

Werbeanzeige (1976)
Print advertisment, 1976

"Exclusive. Explosive. Expensive." This advertising slogan from the nineteen-seventies sums up the characteristics of the Porsche 911 Turbo very appropriately. For more than 30 years it has been regarded as an automobile icon and the ultimate sports car. With its unmatched combination of performance and luxury, the 911 Turbo has matured into a classic that has a special place in Porsche's history.

Seven Turbo generations have now been introduced, and illustrate the Porsche brand's powers of inno-vation more than any other model. As leaders in automobile technology, they have introduced many an innovation to the automobile scene. The Turbo has never departed from the performance principle, or from the policy always pursued by Ferry Porsche: high performance, lower consumption.

Mit dem ersten serienmäßigen Turbo-Sportwagen schwamm Porsche 1974 gegen den Strom. Selbst innerhalb des Unternehmens wurde geargwöhnt, ob angesichts der Ölkrise ein solches Topmodell überhaupt zeitgemäß sei. Die begeisterte Kundschaft zweifelte keine Sekunde. Zu verlockend war die Fahrdynamik des technisch aus dem Rennsport abgeleiteten Hochleistungssportlers, der zudem mit reichlichem Komfort verwöhnte. Zunächst als prestigeträchtige Kleinserie geplant, wurde der Verkaufserfolg des ersten 911 Turbo zur echten Überraschung und verschob die »Grenzen des Wachstums« bei Porsche um ein gutes Stück. Schon während der ersten drei Modelljahre wurden 2.850 Einheiten des 911 Turbo 3.0 produziert.

Ein Erfolgsgeheimnis der 911-Baureihe ist die ständige technische Evolution, die auch den 911 Turbo dem Ideal des perfekten Sportwagens immer näher brachte. Dank Ladeluftkühler erreichte die Motorleistung 1977 die magische Grenze von 300 PS. Eine vom Porsche 917 abgeleitete Bremsanlage sorgte für eine standesgemäße Verzögerung. Mit diesem Paket wurde der 3,3-Liter-Turbo zu einem echten Dauerbrenner, der bis 1989 jährlich in Details verbessert wurde.

RECHTE SEITE: Turbo-lent: Porsche 911 Turbo (Modelljahr 1975)
RIGHT PAGE: *Turbo-lent: Porsche 911 Turbo (model year 1975)*

Schnellstes Serienfahrzeug seiner Zeit: 911 Turbo (Modelljahr 1975)
The fastest production car of its day: Porsche 911 Turbo 3.0 (model year 1975)

Porsche swam against the tide in 1974, when it introduced its first series-production sports car with a turbocharged engine. Even senior company executives were doubtful whether a new top model such as this should be launched midway through an oil crisis. The customers, on the other hand, didn't hesitate for a moment. The dynamic road behavior of this high-performance sports car, with technical features taken directly from motor sport and with a true luxury specification, was simply irresistible. Although the original idea was for a short, prestigious production run, the first 911 Turbo was a remarkable sales success, and caused everyone to rethink the limits of sports-car market growth. During the first three model years, 2,850 911 Turbo 3.0 cars were sold. One of the secrets of the Porsche 911 model line's success is its ongoing technical evolution, which has also helped to bring the 911 Turbo steadily closer to sports-car perfection. In 1977, for instance, charge-air intercooling raised engine output above the magic 300-horsepower barrier. For equally effective braking power, a brake system first developed for the legendary Porsche 917 racing car was adopted. This package kept the 3.3-liter Turbo selling strongly, with

Als Nachfolger ging Anfang der neunziger Jahre ein 911 Turbo an den Start, der eine neue Ära einleitete. Nach über 20 Jahren wurde der »Elfer« gründlich überarbeitet, was sich nicht nur auf die aerodynamische Karosserie beschränkte: 85 Prozent aller Teile der intern 964 genannten Baureihe waren neu. Selbstverständlich präsentierte Porsche auch eine Turbo-Variante, die ab 1990 mit 320 PS beim Händler stand. Zwei Jahre darauf erhielt das Spitzenmodell einen 3,6-Liter-Motor, der mit 360 PS nicht nur deutlich stärker, sondern auch wesentlich verbrauchsärmer war.

Der nächster Turbo-Meilenstein folgte 1995 auf dem Genfer Automobilsalon: Mit dem Turbo der Typenreihe 993 präsentierte Porsche einen Hochleistungssportwagen, der mit technischen Highlights wie Allradantrieb oder Hohlspeichen-Aluminiumfelgen beeindruckte. Sein mit dem Abgas-Kontroll-System OBD II ausgestatteter Biturbo-Motor verblüffte die Fachwelt, als er sich als emissionsärmster Serien-Automobilantrieb der Welt entpuppte.

Die im Januar 2000 folgende Generation des Porsche 911 Turbo (996) krönte die Produktoffensive des

Typ 964: 911 Turbo 3,6 (Modelljahr 1993)
Type 996: 911 Turbo 3,6 (model year 1993)

Typ 993: 911 Turbo 3,6 (model year 1997)
Type 993: 911 Turbo 3,6 (model year 1997)

detail improvements in each model year until 1989. Early in the nineteen-nineties a follow-up model reached the market: a totally new 911 Turbo, known internally as the Type 964. It ushered in a new era: after more than 20 years, the complete 911 model program was extensively revised, with an even more aerodynamic body and no fewer than 85 percent new components. Porsche dealers were naturally given a Turbo version to sell from 1990 on; its engine developed 320 hp. Two years after this, a new 3.6-liter engine was introduced for the top 911 model: with an output of 360 hp, it was not only distinctly more powerful but also significantly more economical.

The next Turbo milestone was reached in 1995, at the Geneva Motor Show. The Type 993 Turbo was a new high-performance sports car with many technical highlights including all-wheel drive and hollow-spoke aluminum wheels. Its twin-turbo engine, equipped with OBD II exhaust emission monitoring equipment, amazed the experts by proving to have lower emission levels than any other production-car engine on the international market.

Zuffenhausener Sportwagenherstellers: Als erster Turbo konnte er mit 5-Gang-Tiptronic S und der Keramik-Verbundscheibenbremse »PCCB« erworben werden. Gegenüber dem Vorgänger verringerte sich der Verbrauch des 420 PS-Triebwerks noch einmal um 18 Prozent auf 12,9 Liter/100 Kilometer (EG-Norm). Möglich wurde dies durch Vierventil-Technik, Wasserkühlung und vor allem dem Einsatz von VarioCam Plus.

Typ 996: Porsche 911 Turbo (Modelljahr 2001)
Type 996: Porsche 911 Turbo (model year 2001)

The next-generation Porsche 911 Turbo (the Type 996), introduced in January 2000, was the spearhead of a product campaign launched by the Zuffenhausen-based carmaker: it was the first Turbo available with 5-speed Tiptronic S transmission and PCCB ceramic disk brakes. Compared with the previous engine, fuel consumption had been reduced on the latest 420-hp unit by a further 18 percent, to an EU standard test-cycle figure of 12.9 liters per 100 kilometers (21.9 UK, 18.2 US mpg). Features contributing to this outstanding result were the use of four valves per cylinder, water cooling and above all "VarioCam Plus" valve gear.

For the 2006 model year, a 911 Turbo based on the latest technological evolution of the 911 model line, the Type 997, was introduced. This was the sixth Turbo generation, and the first gasoline-fueled production car to have a turbocharger with variable turbine geometry (VTG). The new technologies, including controlled all-wheel drive (PTM), the PASM variable damping system and the application of intelligent lightweight construction methods, accompanied a boost in this potent sports car's

Im Modelljahr 2006 folgte mit dem 911 Turbo auf Basis der Generation »997« eine weitere Evolutionsstufe des Technologieträgers. Die inzwischen sechste Turbo-Generation verfügte als erstes Serienautomobil mit Benzinmotor über einen Turbolader mit variabler Turbinengeometrie (VTG). Neue Technologien wie das gesteuerte Allradsystem PTM, das variable Dämpfungssystem PASM und intelligenter Leichtbau ermöglichten einen weiteren Performancesprung des 480 PS starken Sportlers, dessen Verbrauchswerte einmal mehr gesenkt werden konnten.

Noch mehr Dynamik bei niedrigerem Verbrauch ist auch der aktuellsten Turbo-Generation ins Lastenheft geschrieben worden. Herzstück und Höhepunkt des im Herbst 2009 vorgestellten 911 Turbo ist der neue Motor mit 3,8 Liter Hubraum und 500 PS. Das von Grund auf neu konstruierte Triebwerk verfügt über Benzindirekteinspritzung und kann erstmals mit einem Siebengang-Porsche-Doppelkupplungsgetriebe (PDK) kombiniert werden. Mit ihm geht die 911 Turbo-Story weiter.

Typ 997: Porsche 911 Turbo Cabriolet (Modelljahr 2007)
Type 997: Porsche 911 Turbo Cabriolet (2007 model year)

RECHTE SEITE: Der neue Porsche 911 Turbo: deutlich weniger Verbrauch, noch mehr Dynamik
RIGHT PAGE: *The new Porsche 911 Turbo: consumption down significantly, performance up once again*

power output to 480 hp – once again with a reduction in fuel consumption.

Still more dynamic performance and lower fuel consumption were the demands that the latest Turbo model generation had to satisfy. Highspot and key element in the design of the 911 Turbo introduced in the fall of 2009 is the new engine, with a displacement of 3.8 liters and a power output of 500 hp. It's new in every respect, has direct gasoline injection and is available for the first time with a seven-speed Porsche PDK double-clutch transmission. The 911 Turbo story goes on!

		1. GENERATION	2. GENERATION	3. GENERATION	
TYP | TYPE		**TURBO 3.0**	**TURBO 3.3**	**TURBO 3.3**	**TURBO 3.6**
Modellreihe | Internal type number		930	930	964	964
Bauzeitraum/Modelljahr | Model years		1975–1977	1978–1989	1991–1992	1993–1994
Stückzahlen | Quantity built		2874	17831	3871	1437
Leistung | Power output	PS | hp	260	300	320	360
Hubraum | Displacement	cm³	2993	3299	3299	3600
Drehmoment | Torque	Nm	350	430	450	520
Höchstgeschwindigkeit | Top speed	km/h	über | over 250	260	270	280
0–100 km/h ca. | 0–100 kph (app).	s	5,4	5,2	5,2	4,8

4. GENERATION	5. GENERATION	6. GENERATION	7. GENERATION
TURBO	**TURBO**	**TURBO**	**TURBO**
993	996	997 I	997 II
1995–1998	2001–2005	2006–2009	ab 2010
6015	20499	19240	–
408	420	480	500
3600	3600	3600	3800
540	560	620	650
293	305	310	312
4,5	4,2	3,9	3,6

POWERPLAY – DER TRAUM VON DER AUFLADUNG
FORCED ASPIRATION – THE ENGINE DESIGNER'S VISION

POWERPLAY – DER TRAUM VON DER AUFLADUNG
FORCED ASPIRATION – THE ENGINE DESIGNER'S VISION

Beinahe so alt wie der Verbrennungsmotor selbst, ist der Wunsch der Ingenieure nach der »idealen Füllung«, das heißt, der optimalen Verbrennung des Kraftstoff-Luftgemisches. Dabei ist es das Ziel der Techniker, möglichst viel Luft in die Zylinder zu bekommen, damit sie, komprimiert und mit Kraftstoff vermischt, durch Verbrennung einen hohen Arbeitsdruck (sprich: Leistung) erzeugen kann. Hierin liegt der Vorteil von aufgeladenen Motoren. Die Verbrennungsluft wird nicht vom Kolben angesaugt, sondern unter Druck in die Zylinder gepumpt. Kurz: Umso größer der Druck, desto höher die Motorleistung.

Der erste Turbo-Elfer: Porsche 911 Carrera RSR Turbo 2,1 (1974)
The first turbocharged 911: the Porsche 911 Carrera RSR Turbo 2.1 (1974)

Almost as old as the internal combustion engine itself is the engineers' wish for its cylinders to be filled as efficiently as possible: the "ideal charge" that permits smooth, rapid combustion of the fuel-air mixture. The aim is to draw as much air as possible into the cylinders, mix it with fuel, compress it and achieve a high mean effective pressure (and therefore power output) when combustion takes place. If the air is simply drawn in by the pistons, this is known as natural aspiration. But when it is pumped into the cylinders at a higher pressure, we speak of forced aspiration or, if a mechanically driven pump is used, of supercharging. Other things being equal, the higher this boost pressure, the higher the power output.

Als Pionier der Motorenaufladung gilt der Schweizer Ingenieur Alfred Büchi, der sich schon 1905 ein Patent für einen mittels Turbine und Verdichter aufgeladenen Viertaktmotor sicherte. Bei diesem Prinzip der Leistungssteigerung werden die Luftverdichter des Turboladers vom Abgasstrom angetrieben, dessen hohe Energie normalerweise ungenutzt bleibt. Diese Innovation setzte Büchi erfolgreich bei Schiffsdieselmotoren ein, deren Leistung er mittels Abgas-Turbolader um 40 Prozent steigern konnte. Später waren es dann Eisenbahnen und Lastwagen, deren Dieselantriebe mit Turboladern versehen wurden.

Der seit den zwanziger Jahren in der Automobiltechnik begangene Weg war zunächst die Motorenaufladung mittels Kompressor, das heißt eines mechanischen Drehkolben-Verdichters, der vom Motor über Ketten-, Riemen- oder Zahnradgetriebe angetrieben wurde. Die nach den Erfindern dieses Konstruktionsprinzips, den Gebrüdern Philander und Francis Roots, auch »Roots-Gebläse« genannten Lader hatten zwei gegenläufige Rotoren, deren keulenförmige Flügel wechselweise ineinander greifen und die komprimierte Verbrennungsluft in den Motor hineindrücken. Diese

Kompressormotor des Mercedes 2-Liter-Rennwagens »Monza« (1924)
Supercharged engine of the Mercedes "Monza" 2-liter racing car (1924)

Forced aspiration was pioneered by the Swiss engineer Alfred Büchi, who submitted a patent application as early as 1905 for a four-cycle engine supplied with air by a "turbocharger", a rotary device with a turbine and an impeller. Exhaust gas from the engine, a source of energy that normally escaped unused to the atmosphere, was directed against the turbine blades, and the impeller on the same shaft forced air into the engine's cylinders at more than atmospheric pressure. Büchi applied his invention successfully to ships' diesel engines, and was able to increase their power output by as much as 40 percent. Later, diesel engines for locomotives and trucks were also turbocharged.

Automobile engineering initially pursued a different path: in the nineteen-twenties some car engines were supercharged using a rotary compressor driven from the engine by chain, belt or gears. The "Roots blower", as this type of supercharger was familiarly known, was invented by the brothers Philander and Francis Roots. It has two contra-rotating rotors, with intersecting lobes that compress the combustion air and force it into the cylinders. These "blowers" were used in particular on sports-car and racing engines,

Ferdinand Porsche und
der von ihm konstruierte
Mercedes »Monza«-Renn-
wagen bei Probefahrten im
September 1924
Ferdinand Porsche with the
Mercedes "Monza" racing
car he designed (during
trials in September 1924)

»Gebläse« wurden vor allem in Sport- und Rennwagen verwendet, denn die aufgeladenen Motoren kamen – bei gleicher Leistung – mit weniger Hubraum aus und konnten somit ihren Größen- und Gewichtsvorteil ausspielen.

Die Erfahrungen von Porsche mit diesem Prinzip der Motoraufladung reichen zurück bis in die zweite Hälfte der zwanziger Jahre, als unter Leitung von Professor Ferdinand Porsche die legendären Mercedes-Benz Kompressor-Sportwagen entwickelt wurden. Auch der Motor des 1933 vom Konstruktionsbüro Porsche entwickelten Auto Union Grand-Prix-Rennwagens Typ 22 wurde durch einen Kompressor beatmet. Sein aufgeladener 16-Zylinder-Mittelmotor machte den so genannten »P-Rennwagen« (P für Porsche) zu einem der dominierenden Rennwagen seiner Zeit.

Für Ferry Porsche war es daher nur naheliegend, dass er Ende der dreißiger Jahre auch die Leistung seines Käfer-Prototypen VW39-Cabriolet mit einem Kompressor steigerte. Eine Idee, die ihn zeitlebens nicht mehr loslassen sollte. Auch die erste große Nachkriegs-

Ferdinand Porsche betrachtet den 16-Zylinder-Kompressormotor im Auto-Union-Rennwagen (Porsche Typ 22)
Ferdinand Porsche examining the supercharged 16-cylinder engine in the Auto Union racing car (Porsche Type 22)

and enabled the same power to be obtained from an engine of smaller displacement and lower weight. Porsche's experience with this forced aspiration principle goes back to the late nineteen-twenties, when development of the legendary Mercedes-Benz "Kompressor" sports cars was in the hands of Professor Ferdinand Porsche. The 16-cylinder engine for the Auto Union Type 22 Grand Prix racing car developed in 1933 by the Porsche Design Office was supercharged, and made this "P" (for Porsche) mid-engine design one of the dominant racing cars of its era.

For Ferry Porsche at the end of the nineteen-thirties it was no more than a logical step to boost the power output of his VW 39 "Beetle" convertible prototype by installing a supercharger. He remained loyal to this principle later: Porsche's first major post-war project, the Type 360 "Cisitalia" Grand Prix race car, had a supercharged twelve-cylinder engine that developed 385 horsepower from a displacement of only 1.5 liters.

Aus 1,5 Liter Hubraum
holte der 1947 konstruierte
Kompressor-Motor des
Typ 360 beeindruckende
385 PS
From a displacement of
1.5 liters, the supercharged
engine for the Type 360,
designed in 1947,
developed an impressive
385 horsepower

entwicklung von Porsche, der Grand-Prix-Rennwagen Typ 360 »Cisitalia«, erhielt einen Kompressor-Motor, dessen zwölf Zylinder aus nur 1,5 Liter Hubraum eine Leistung von 385 PS schöpften.

Bei den Personenwagen blieben die technisch aufwändigen Kompressor-Motoren allerdings eine seltene Ausnahme, denn aufgrund ihrer Wirkungsweise arbeiteten die Kompressoren erst ab einer größeren Luftmenge effektiv und waren zudem relativ voluminös und schwer. Aus diesem Grund interessierten sich die Automobilingenieure schon bald wieder für die von Alfred Büchi erdachte Idee des leichten und kompakten Abgas-Turboladers. Es galt jedoch das Problem zu lösen, den Turbolader an die verschiedenen Fahrzustände anzupassen, etwa an den Übergang vom Beschleunigen in den Schubbetrieb oder während des Schaltvorgangs. Vor diesem Hintergrund waren es denn zunächst auch Schiffs- und Flugmotoren, deren Motoren dank ihrer gleichmäßigen Drehzahlen für den Turbolader geeignet waren.

In den fünfziger Jahren experimentierten dann amerikanische Rennteams mit Turbomotoren, die

Alfred Büchi patentierte 1905 eine Verbundmaschine aus Achtzylinder-Sternmotor und einer Abgasturbine. *In 1905 Alfred Büchi patented a compound eight-cylinder radial engine with exhaust-driven turbine.*

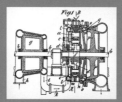

Due to its technical complexity, the supercharger remained an exception on the passenger-car scene; it was relatively large and heavy, another disadvantage being that it only operated efficiently when the airflow was fairly high. These were reasons enough for car designers to take a closer look at the lighter, more compact turbocharger invented by Alfred Büchi, especially since it was driven by the exhaust gas rather than by a mechanical transmission. Problems nonetheless remained to be solved; for instance the turbocharged engine's response during transition from acceleration to coasting or during gear shifts. For a long time, the turbocharger was considered more suitable for marine and aircraft engines that operated for long periods at a constant speed.

In the nineteen-fifties, American motor-sport teams experimented with turbocharged engines: their far from smooth power flow suited them best to the country's oval racetracks, where engine speeds were more or less constant. Encouraged by these attempts, the American automobile corporation General Motors decided to develop turbocharged engines for passenger cars in the early nineteen-

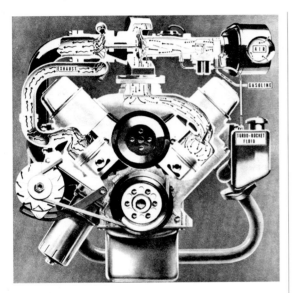

Der 3,5-Liter V8-Motor des
Oldmobile F-85 »Jetfire«
aus dem Jahr 1961
*The 3.5-liter V8 engine from
the Oldmobile F-85 "Jetfire",
1961*

Schnittzeichnung des
aufgeladenen Motors des
Chevrolet Corvair Monza
aus dem Jahr 1962
*Sectioned drawing of
the turbocharged engine
of the Chevrolet Monza
from 1962*

aufgrund ihrer extremen Leistungscharakteristik nur bei Ovalrennen eingesetzt werden konnten, da diese mit relativ konstanter Drehzahl gefahren wurden. Davon inspiriert, versuchte sich der amerikanische Automobilkonzern General Motors zu Beginn der sechziger Jahre an Turbo-Personenwagen. Doch die eher schlicht konstruierten Turbo-Triebwerke der Modelle Oldsmobile Turbo Jetfire und Chevrolet Corvair Monza waren von einer wirklichen Marktreife noch so weit entfernt, dass GM das Projekt nach kurzer Zeit wieder einstellte.

In Europa war es der Schweizer Ex-Rennfahrer und Ingenieur Michael May, der das Turbo-Prinzip auf die Straße brachte. Zu Beginn der siebziger Jahre bot er ein Turbo-Kit für den Ford Capri an, das die Leistung des robusten 2,3-Liter-Sechszylinders auf 180 PS steigerte. Auf dieses Triebwerk wurde auch der damalige Porsche-Entwicklungschef Ferdinand Piëch aufmerksam, der bereits 1969 auf dem Prüfstand ein 2-Liter-Triebwerk des 911 mit einem Turbolader hatte versehen lassen. Nachdem diese Versuche mit dem Porsche-Sechszylinder nur mäßig erfolgreich verlaufen waren, ließ Piëch im Firmenauftrag einen »May-Capri«

Ford Capri »Turbo May« (1971)
Ford Capri "Turbo May", 1971

sixties. Fairly simple designs appeared in the Oldsmobile Turbo Jetfire and Chevrolet Corvair Monza, but they were so far removed from genuine market maturity that GM abandoned the project after a short time.

One of the pioneers of turbocharging for road cars in Europe was the Swiss engineer and ex-racing driver Michael May. In the early nineteen-seventies he began to sell an add-on turbocharging kit for the Ford Capri which boosted the output of the car's sturdy 2.3-liter six-cylinder engine to 180 hp. Porsche's development director at that time was Ferdinand Piëch, who had run a turbocharged two-liter 911 engine on the test rig as early as 1969. These trials with the modified Porsche six-cylinder engine were only moderately successful, and at Piëch's request the company therefore ordered a "May-Capri" from the Stuttgart Ford dealer Schwabengarage. It was driven on the test circuit at Porsche's development center in Weissach, but the simple intake-side boost pressure control system gave very poor results: the car was unpredictable to drive, and was sold off soon after. Porsche's engineers retained their interest in

bei der Stuttgarter Schwabengarage anschaffen.
Doch angesichts der simplen ansaugseitigen Lade-
druckregelung fiel dessen Fahrererprobung auf dem
Weissacher Testgelände so ernüchternd aus, dass
der kapriziös zu fahrende Wagen schon bald wieder
verkauft wurde. Die Porsche-Techniker schlugen ihrem
Chef daraufhin vor, nach einem passenden Abgas-
Turbolader zu fahnden, der auch für die speziellen
Anforderungen eines Boxermotors geeignet war.

Auf der Suche nach einem passenden Lader wurden
die Ingenieure 1971 bei der Firma Kühnle, Kopp &
Kausch (KKK) fündig, die bereits einige Erfahrung mit
Diesel-Turboladern besaß. Auf Benzinmotoren ließ sich
diese Technik ohne weiteres jedoch nicht übertragen.
Zunächst mussten zahlreiche Probleme gelöst werden:
Während die abgasseitigen Temperaturen von Diesel-
motoren nur rund 700 Grad Celsius erreichten, waren
es beim Porsche-Boxermotor über 900 Grad Celsius,
was die Grauguss-Gehäuse der Turbinen nicht ver-
trugen. Hinzu kamen Probleme bei der Abdichtung und
Schmierung der Lager, da eine der beiden Turbinen
im heißen Abgasstrom lag, während die andere kühle
Außenluft ansaugte. Mit herkömmlichen Kugellagern

Turbo-Pionier: Der Porsche-
Motorenkonstrukteur
Hans Mezger (1970)
*Turbo pioneer: Porsche
engine designer
Hans Mezger (1970)*

the principle, however, and asked their director to
look for a turbocharger that would suit the specific
requirements of a horizontally-opposed engine as
used in the 911.

The search ended in 1971 with a product from the
Kühnle, Kopp & Kausch (KKK) company, which already
had considerable experience of turbocharging diesel
engines. But even then, many problems had to be
tackled to make the technology suitable for gasoline
engines. Diesel-engine exhaust gas, for example, only
reaches peak temperatures of about 700 degrees
Celsius, but the equivalent figure on the Porsche
flat-six engine was more than 900 degrees – too much
for the KKK turbocharger's gray cast iron housing.
There were also difficulties in sealing and lubricating
the bearings, since the turbine was located in the
hot exhaust gas, whereas the impeller at the other
end of the shaft was surrounded by cool intake air.
Conventional ball bearings had no chance of withstanding the heat without their seals beginning to
leak; "floating" plain bearings lubricated directly from
the engine oil circuit were therefore adopted. This led
to a further problem: on the low-slung Porsche engine

war die geforderte Druckdichte und Hitze-Verträglich-keit nicht zu erreichen, so dass man »schwimmende« Gleitlager verwendete, die direkt vom Ölkreislauf des Motors versorgt wurden. Darin lag auch schon die nächste Schwierigkeit: Da der flache Boxermotor auf dem Weg vom Lader in den Öltank und in das Kurbel-gehäuse kein Gefälle hatte, musste das Öl mittels spe-ziell entwickelter Ventile und einer Rückförderpumpe transportiert werden. Ein weiteres Ziel bestand darin, den Turbolader so kompakt wie möglich zu halten. Der Grund hierfür lag nicht allein an den knappen Platz-verhältnissen im Motorraum. Aufgrund der geringeren Massenträgheit sprach grundsätzlich eine kleine Tur-bine bei niedrigen Drehzahlen schneller an, was sich positiv auf die Elastizität des Motors auswirkte.

Das Hauptproblem der Turbo-Motoren bestand jedoch darin, die geförderte Luftmenge an die Bedingungen des Fahrens anzupassen, sprich das vom Ladedruck abhängige Ansprechverhalten beim Gasgeben oder -wegnehmen. Die ständig im Abgasstrom laufende Verdichter-Turbine lieferte nicht nur meist mehr Ladedruck als gebraucht wurde, sondern reagierte auch deutlich verzögert auf Veränderungen der Gas-

Der Porsche-
Vorstandsvorsitzende
Dr. Ernst Fuhrmann
*Dr. Ernst Fuhrmann,
Chairman of the Porsche
Board of Managenent*

the oil from the turbocharger was unable to flow back to the oil tank and crankcase by gravity. Special valves and a return-flow pump had to be developed. The designers also wanted the turbocharger to be as compact as possible, not only because space under the Porsche 911's engine hood was limited, but also because the lower moment of inertia of a small turbine improves its response at low engine speeds and therefore makes the engine more flexible.

The first turbocharged car engines faced a fundamental problem: how to vary the air delivery volume quickly when the driving situation changed. This called for a rapid variation in boost pressure whenever the driver pressed the gas pedal down or released it. Since it rotated in a constant exhaust gas flow, the turbine normally provided more boost pressure than was actually needed, and reacted only sluggishly to accelerator pedal movements and changes in engine speed. This much-criticized delay in responding to the driver's wishes for more power became known as "turbo lag". To eliminate the problem, Porsche's engineers explored a new path: instead of the conventional method of controlling boost pressure on the intake side, they

pedalstellung und Motordrehzahl – das viel zitierte »Turbo-Loch«. Zur Lösung dieses Problems gingen die Porsche-Ingenieure einen neuen Weg: Statt der herkömmlichen ansaugseitigen Regelung entwickelten sie eine abgasseitige Steuerung des Ladedrucks. Im Teillast- oder Schubbetrieb wurde unerwünschter Überdruck verhindert, indem überschüssige Auspuffgase nicht mehr durch die Abgasturbine, sondern über eine Entlastungsleitung (auch »Bypass« genannt) geleitet wurden. Wenn beim Beschleunigen wieder Ladedruck benötigt wurde, schloss sich das Bypass-Ventil, und die Turbine konnte im Abgasstrom ihre volle Arbeitsleistung entwickeln.

developed a means of performing this task on the exhaust side of the engine. This avoided excess pressure at part load or when coasting, by diverting the unwanted amount of exhaust gas away from the turbine and through a bypass line. As soon as more boost pressure was needed, for instance when accelerating, the bypass valve closed and the turbine developed its full power.

Motorenprüfstand im Porsche Entwicklungszentrum Weissach
Engine test bench at Porsche's Development Center in Weissach

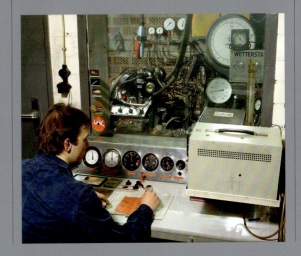

DER TURBO IM RENNSPORT

Trotz aller anfänglichen Probleme verliefen die Versuche mit den ersten Turbomotoren so viel ver-
sprechend, dass bei Porsche schon bald der Gedanke
eines Motorsporteinsatzes der neuen Technologie
reifte. Als geeignete Rennserie bot sich der nordame-
rikanische Canadian-American Challenge Cup (CanAm)
an, dessen liberales Regelwerk keine Hubraumlimi-
tierung von aufgeladenen Motoren verlangte. Porsche
war in der CanAm-Serie mit dem 917 PA bereits seit
1969 am Start, um für die gemeinsame US-Vertriebs-
gesellschaft von Porsche und Volkswagen Werbung
zu machen. Und mit dem Porsche 917/10 stand 1971
eine ideale Ausgangsbasis bereit, um einen turbo-
geladenen Motor im Renneinsatz zu erproben.

Unter der Regie von Hans Mezger und Valentin
Schäffer wurde der 4,5-Liter-Zwölfzylinder Typ 912
mit zwei Eberspächer-Turboladern ausgestattet, deren
überschüssige Energie durch ein »Wastegate«-Ventil in
den Auspufftrakt geleitet wurde. Nach arbeitsreichen
Monaten der Erprobung auf der Weissacher Teststrecke wurde der 917/10 in der Can-Am-Saison 1972

LINKE SEITE: Willibald
Kauhsen auf Porsche
917/10 beim Interserie-
Lauf des »Int. ADAC
300 km Rennen« auf dem
Nürburgring 1973
LEFT PAGE: *Willibald
Kauhsen driving the
Porsche 917/10 during
the Interseries ADAC
300-kilometer race at the
Nurburg Ring in 1973*

Prüfstandstest des Turbo-
motors für den Porsche Typ
917/10 in Weissach 1971
*Turbocharged engine rig
test for the Porsche Type
917/10 in Weissach, 1971*

THE TURBOCHARGER IN MOTOR SPORT

Despite initial problems, tests with the first turbocharged engines were so promising that Porsche
began to think about trying out the new technology on
the racetrack. The Canadian-American Challenge Cup
(CanAm) series seemed ideal for the purpose, since
its rules were not too restrictive, and turbocharged
engines were not subject to a displacement limit.
Porsche first entered the CanAm series in 1969
with the 917 PA, the aim being to publicize the joint
Porsche and Volkswagen sales organization in the
USA. By 1971 the Porsche 917/10 was available, an
ideal car for testing the turbocharged engine in racing
conditions.

Hans Mezger and Valentin Schäffer were in charge of
equipping the 4.5-liter, twelve-cylinder Type 912 with
two Eberspächer turbochargers; excess energy was
diverted back into the exhaust pipe by a "waste gate"
valve. After several months of intensive testing on
Porsche's high-speed track in Weissach, the 917/10
was entered by the Penske racing team for 1972
CanAm series events. Its initial power output was

unter Regie des Penske-Rennteams an den Start geschickt. Mit einer Leistung von anfänglich 850 PS, die nach einer Hubraumerhöhung auf 1000 PS anstieg, wurde der Porsche 917/10 zum dominierenden Rennwagen in der CanAm. Nach Siegen in Road Atlanta, Mid Ohio, Elkhart Lake, Laguna Seca und Riverside gewann er unangefochten die CanAm-Meisterschaft. Und auch im europäischen Pendant, der Interserie, war der Turbo-917 höchst erfolgreich. Er siegte nicht nur auf Anhieb auf dem Hockenheimer Motodrom, sondern holte auch hier den Meistertitel.

Für die Saison 1973 konstruierte Porsche mit dem 917/30 nicht nur ein weitgehend neues Auto, sondern steigerte auch den Hubraum des Zwölfzylinders von 5 auf 5,4 Liter. Mit je nach Ladedruck bis zu 1200 PS war der 800 Kilogramm leichte Porsche 917/30 der stärkste Rennwagen, der jemals bei einem Rundstreckenrennen an den Start ging. Seine Fahrleistungen lassen noch heute staunen: Von Null auf Hundert beschleunigte er in 2,4 Sekunden, die 200 Stundenkilometer-Marke wurde nach 5,6 Sekunden durchbrochen, und eine Geschwindigkeit von 300 km/h war nach nur 11,3 Sekunden erreicht. Wie im Vorjahr,

Porsche-Rennmechaniker Achim Stolz bei der Montage des 12-Zylinder-Turbomotors (1972/73) *Porsche competition department mechanic Achim Stolz assembling the 12-cylinder turbocharged engine (1972/73)*

LINKE SEITE: Porsche 917/30 beim CanAm-Lauf in Riverside, USA (1973) **LEFT PAGE:** *Porsche 917/30 cars in the CanAm race in Riverside, USA (1973)*

850 hp, rising to 1000 hp when the engine size was increased. The Porsche 917/10 dominated the CanAm race season, and walked away with the championship title after wins in Road Atlanta, Mid Ohio, Elkhart Lake, Laguna Seca and Riverside. The turbocharged Type 917 was also successful In the equivalent European Interseries. It won on its first appearance at the Motodrome in Hockenheim and went on to take the European championship title.

For 1973, Porsche designed the 917/30, a largely new car with the engine increased in size from 5 to 5.4 liters. Depending on turbocharger boost pressure, this car, which weighted only 800 kilograms, had up to 1200 horsepower at its disposal. It could reach 100 kilometers an hour (62 mph) from a standing start in 2.4 seconds, break the 200-kph barrier in 5.6 seconds, and exceed 300 kph in only 11.3 seconds – unbelievable figures that made it the most potent car ever to appear on the racing circuit. As in the previous season, the big-engined Porsche wiped the floor with its rivals. The 917/30 won the CanAm championship with such consummate ease that the organizers changed the rules at short notice

LINKE SEITE: Porsche
917/10 auf der Weissacher
Teststrecke (1971)
LEFT PAGE: *Porsche*
917/10 at the test track
in Weissach, 1971

Porsche 917/30 Spyder
1973 im Weissacher
Entwicklungszentrum
Porsche 917/30 Spyder at
the Weissach Development
Center, 1973

Weltrekord: Im 917/30 fuhr
Mark Donohue 1975 ein
Durchschnittstempo von
355,86 km/h
*World record: In 1975, Mark
Donohue lapped the circuit
at an average speed of
355.86 kph (221.12 mph)*

zeigte sich Porsche auch 1973 den Hubraumriesen der Konkurrenz überlegen. Der 917/30 gewann die CanAm-Meisterschaft so unangefochten, dass das Reglement der Serie kurzfristig geändert wurde, um den übermächtigen Porsche von einer weiteren Teilnahme in der Saison auszuschließen. Bevor der Porsche 917/30 endgültig ins Museum wanderte, machte er 1975 noch einmal nachhaltig auf sich aufmerksam: Auf dem Rundkurs von Talladega, USA, stellte der Rennfahrer Mark Donohue mit ihm einen Rundenweltrekord auf. Durch die Verwendung von Ladeluftkühlern war die Leistung des auch aerodynamisch optimierten 917/30 auf 1.500 PS angestiegen, so dass der Spyder ein Rekord-Durchschnittstempo von 355,86 km/h erzielte.

Das 1972/73 in der CanAm gesammelte Know-how sollte nicht lange ungenutzt bleiben. Als 1974 ein neues Reglement für »Produktionswagen« der Gruppe 5 angekündigt wurde, dachten die Porsche-Ingenieure sofort an eine Turbo-Version des zuverlässigen, aber inzwischen leistungsmäßig unterlegenen 911 Carrera 3.0 RSR. Zwar belegte das Regelwerk den Hubraum von Turbo-Motoren mit einem Handicap-Faktor, doch

Das 1200 PS-Triebwerk des Typ 917/30
The Type 917/30's 1200-hp engine

to exclude the mighty Porsche from the rest of the season's races. But in 1975, before the Porsche 917/30 finally made its way into the museum, it made the headlines one more time: on the Talladega racetrack in the USA, driver Mark Donohue set a new world circuit racing speed record. Charge-air intercoolers boosted power output to an even more impressive 1500 hp, and with the benefit of various aerodynamic tweaks to the body, the 917/30 Spyder lapped the circuit at the record average speed of 355.86 kph (221.12 mph).

The know-how accumulated in the 1972 and 1973 CanAm seasons was soon put to good use. In the following year, a new set of rules for Group 5 "production cars" was announced, and Porsche's engineers immediately started to plan a turbocharged version of their 911 Carrera 3.0 RSR, which was reliable but down on power compared with its rivals. Although the rules imposed a handicap factor on cars with turbocharged engines, this was felt to be negligible compared with the power hike expected from a turbocharged 911. A design study for a series-production 911 Turbo had in fact already been

dies schien angesichts der zu erwartenden Leistungs-
fähigkeit eines Turbo-Elfers kein Hindernis. Umso
mehr vor dem Hintergrund, dass man bereits 1973 die
Studie einer Serienversion des 911 Turbo vorgestellt
hatte, und den Rennsport einmal mehr zur intensiven
Erprobung nutzen wollte.

Für den neuen Rennwagen wurde ein 2142-Kubikzenti-
meter-Triebwerk konstruiert, das aus Gewichtsgründen
ein Kurbelgehäuse aus Magnesium erhielt. Die Ingenieure nutzten viele Erfahrungen aus dem CanAm-Pro-
jekt, so dass wie schon beim 917/30 neben den Pleuel
auch die Einlassventile aus Titan gefertigt wurden.
Zur Leistungssteigerung diente ein KKK-Turbolader,
der nach einigen Fahrversuchen von einem Ladeluftkühler ergänzt wurde. Dieser wurde unter dem mäch-
tigen Heckflügel platziert und durch NACA-Lufteinlässe
mit Kaltluft versorgt. Das Resultat überzeugte: Mit bis
zu 500 PS bei 1,5 bar Ladedruck zeigte der 911 Carrera RSR Turbo 2.1 eindrücklich das Leistungspotenzial des Sechszylinder-Boxermotors. In 3,2 Sekunden
beschleunigte der Wagen auf 100 km/h, und in
8,8 Sekunden auf 200 km/h.

Das Kraftwerk: 2,1-Liter-
Sechszylinder-Turbo
*The power source:
a 2.1-liter six-cylinder
turbocharged engine*

announced, and as on previous occasions intensive
trials in racing conditions were planned.

A 2142-cc engine was built for the new race car,
with a magnesium crankcase to save weight. The
engineers were able to use a lot of the know-how
gathered from the CanAm series: as on the 917/30,
for instance, the conrods and the inlet valves were
both of titanium. Power output was boosted by a
KKK turbocharger, to which an intercooler was added
after a series of road trials. It was located under the
massive rear wing, and supplied with cool air through
NACA intake ducts. The results were impressive: with
up to 500 horsepower available at a boost pressure
of 1.5 bar, the 911 Carrera RSR Turbo 2.1 showed
what performance potential could still be obtained
from the flat-six engine. The car accelerated from a
standing start to 100 kph (62 mph) in 3.2 seconds,
and rocketed past the 200 kph (124 mph) mark in
8.8 seconds.

This Turbo for the racetrack was only used during the
1974 season, since in 1975 the FIA postponed the
anticipated "silhouette formula" for a further year.

2 Meter breit und 500 PS
stark: Porsche 911 Carrera
RSR Turbo 2.1
*2 meters wide with a 500
horsepower engine: Porsche
911 Carrera RSR Turbo 2.1*

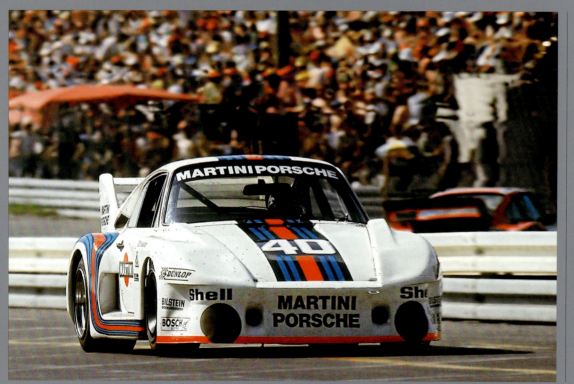

Aus dem Porsche 935
wurde ein Modell für die
kleine Division der DRM
abgeleitet: 935/2.0 »Baby«
*From the Porsche 935 a
model for use in the two-
liter division was developed:
935/2.0 "Baby"*

Im Rennsport eingesetzt wurde der Renn-Turbo jedoch nur im Jahr 1974, da die FIA die für 1975 erwartete »Silhouette-Formel« um ein weiteres Jahr verschob. Mit einem zweiten Platz in Le Mans und Watkins Glen ging er in die Porsche-Renngeschichte ein und lieferte wichtige Erkenntnisse für die Serienversion des 911 Turbo.

Auf dessen Basis kehrte das Turbo-Prinzip 1976 in Gestalt des Porsche 935 auf die internationalen Rennstrecken zurück. Seine Kombination aus Leichtbau, Aerodynamik und standfesten 590 Turbo-PS machten den 935 bis in die achtziger Jahre hinein zu einem der erfolgreichsten Langstreckenrennwagen überhaupt. Nach fünfjähriger Unterbrechung gewann Porsche mit ihm 1976 wieder die Marken-Weltmeisterschaft.

Sein breites Einsatzspektrum zeigte der 935 zudem in Gestalt verschiedener Sonderversionen. In der kleinen Division der Deutschen Rennsportmeisterschaft bis zwei Liter Motorvolumen bewies der 935/2.0 »Baby« im Jahr 1977, dass Porsche nicht nur in großen Hubraumklassen siegen konnte. Sein reglementbedingt auf 1,425 Liter Hubraum reduzierter Turbo-Motor

Porsche 935 (Ickx/Maas) bei den 6 Stunden von Dijon 1976
Porsche 935 (Ickx/Maas) at the 6-hour race in Dijon, 1976

Nonetheless, the car earned an honorable mention in Porsche's motor-sport history with second places in Le Mans and Watkins Glen, and supplied plenty of useful data for the series-production version of the 911 Turbo.

This was the basic approach in 1976, when the turbocharger principle returned to the international racing scene in the guise of the Porsche 935. With its combination of lightweight construction, good aerodynamics and a reliable turbocharged engine delivering 590 horsepower, the 935 was one of the most successful long-distance racing cars of all time, and continued to win races until the early nineteen-eighties, including the manufacturers' world championship in 1976, after a five-year break. Various special versions demonstrated the 935's full motor-sport potential. In the small-engine division (up to 2 liters) of the German sports-car championship, the "baby" 935/2.0 took the title in 1977 and proved that Porsche was not only capable of winning in the larger engine categories. Although reduced to a displacement of only 1425 cc to comply with the rules, the turbocharged engine nonetheless developed 380 hp at 8200 rpm. In 1978, Porsche returned to

Seine Langheck-Karosserie
brachte dem 935/78 den
Spitznamen »Moby Dick« ein
*The long-tailed body earned
the 935/78 the nickname
"Moby Dick"*

RECHTE SEITE: Der Hubraum
des 935/2.0 »Baby« musste
auf 1.425 ccm reduziert
werden
RIGHT PAGE: *The displacement
of the 935/2.0 "Baby" had to
be reduced to 1425 cc*

leistete immerhin 380 PS bei 8.200 /min. Mit dem gewaltigen 935/78 »Moby Dick« kehrte Porsche 1978 noch einmal in die Langstrecken-WM zurück. Mit wassergekühlten Vierventil-Zylinderköpfen ging der liebevoll »Moby Dick« genannte Wagen als stärkster 911 aller Zeiten in die Porsche-Geschichte ein und war auf der Rennstrecke als seriennaher Sportwagen sogar stärker als reinrassige Sport-Prototypen. Aus 3,2 Liter Hubraum holte er dank Bi-Turbo-Aufladung 845 PS – genug für eine Höchstgeschwindigkeit von 366 km/h.

Auch bei anderen Rennwagentypen blieb Porsche dem Turbo-Prinzip treu. Aufgeladene Neunelfer wie der Gruppe 4-Produktionswagen Typ 934 dienten ab 1976 vielen Privatrennfahrern als zuverlässiges und siegfähiges Sportgerät. Das Werksteam beteiligte sich 1976 parallel dazu mit dem Porsche 936 Spyder an der Sportwagen-Weltmeisterschaft in der Gruppe 6. Charakteristisches Merkmal des offenen Rennwagens war die große Airbox hinter dem Cockpit, durch die der Ladeluftkühler des 2,1-Liter-Turbomotors mit Kühlluft versorgt wurde. Auch dieses Projekt wurde ein Erfolg: Nach nur vier von sieben Rennen sicherte sich

Breitensportler: Porsche 934 (1975) *Popular among private motor-sport entrants too: the Porsche 934 (1975)*

RECHTE SEITE: Der erste Porsche 936/76, Spitzname »schwarze Witwe« (1976) **RIGHT PAGE:** The first Porsche 936/76, nickname "Black Widow", 1976

long-distance world championship racing with the monumental 935/78, soon affectionately nicknamed "Moby Dick." With its water-cooled cylinder heads and four valves per cylinder, this car has its place in the Porsche chronicles as the most powerful 911 ever built. Although a near-series sports car, it was more powerful on the racetrack than many a sports-car prototype. Thanks to twin turbochargers, the 3.2-liter engine developed 845 hp – sufficient for a top speed of 366 kph (227 mph).

Porsche remained loyal to the turbocharging principle for other racing cars too. From 1976 on, turbocharged 911s such as the Type 934 Group 4 production model served many a private entrant well as reliable cars with race-winning potential. In 1976 the factory team also entered the Porsche 936 Spyder in parallel for world sports-car championship events, in the Group 6 category. A characteristic feature of this open sports racing car was the large airbox behind the cockpit, through which the 2.1-liter turbocharged engine was supplied with cooling air. This project was also crowned with success: the 936 made sure of the world championship title by winning four of the seven races.

Der Porsche 936 Spyder wurde dreimal Gesamtsieger in Le Mans. 1977 siegte das Porsche-Werksteam Ickx/Barth/Haywood
The Porsche 936 Spyder was the overall winner in Le Mans three times. In 1977 the Porsche factory team's victorious car was driven by Ickx/Barth/Haywood

RECHTE SEITE: Le Mans-Sieger 1981 wurden Jacky Ickx und Derek Bell auf dem 620-PS starken Porsche 936/81 Spyder
RIGHT PAGE: *Le Mans winners in 1981: Jacky Ickx and Derek Bell drove the 620-horsepower Porsche 936/81 Spyder*

Turbo & Transaxle: Porsche
924 Carrera GT »Le Mans«
(1980)
*Turbo and transaxle:
Porsche 924 Carrera GT
"Le Mans" (1980)*

36
BOSS
PORSCHE
Shell
DUNLOP
TELETRON
BILSTEIN
BOSCH
Turbolader

der 936 den WM-Sieg. Und auch in Le Mans zeigte sich der 936 als ein echter Siegertyp: 1976, 1977 und 1981 holte er den Gesamtsieg des Langstreckenklassikers nach Zuffenhausen.

Dass ein Turbolader auch Vierzylindermotoren Flügel verlieh, bewiesen die Rennversionen der Baureihe 924/944. Vom Typ 924 Carrera GT »Le Mans« schickte Porsche 1980 gleich drei Transaxle-Rennwagen nach Le Mans. Mit 320 PS lag ein Gesamtsieg zwar außer Reichweite, doch konnten einmal mehr wichtige Erkenntnisse für die Serienproduktion gesammelt werden. Dies galt auch für den 924 GTP »Le Mans«, dessen Leistung 1981 dank Vierventil-Turbo und vollelektronischer Einspritzung auf 410 PS anstieg. Walter Röhrl und Jürgen Barth erreichten mit ihm nicht nur den siebten Gesamtrang, sondern gewannen auch den Preis für die kürzeste Boxenstandzeit.

Ein weiterer Meilenstein der Porsche-Turbo-Rennwagen war die Teilnahme des Typ 956 in der Langstrecken-Weltmeisterschaft der Gruppe C. Als erster Porsche-Rennwagen mit Monocoque-Chassis und Groundeffekt erzielte er 1982 nicht nur auf Anhieb einen Dreifach-

Der 2,6-Liter-Turbo beschleunigte den 956 auf bis zu 360 km/h
The 2.6-liter turbocharged engine propelled the 956 up to 360 kph (224 mph)

LINKE SEITE: Die 1-2-3 Le Mans-Siegerwagen Typ 956 C auf der Weissacher Teststrecke (1982)
LEFT PAGE: *The Type 956 C that took the first three places in Le Mans, seen on the Weissach test track (1982)*

In Le Mans too, the 936 demonstrated its winning qualities; the manufacturer was able to return home to Zuffenhausen in triumph with overall wins in this classic long-distance race in 1976, 1977 and 1981.

That even four-cylinder engines could soar to new heights when turbocharged was shown by the racing versions of the Porsche 924/944 model line. In 1980, Porsche sent three Type 924 Carrera GTP cars to Le Mans. Like all the cars in this model line, drive to the rear wheels was by transaxle. The available power output of 320 hp ruled out the prospect of an overall win, but once again useful information was acquired for use on production cars. The same applied to the 944 GTP "Le Mans" in 1981, though in this season the turbocharged engine had four valves per cylinder and full electronic fuel injection, so that its power output went up to 410 hp. Walter Röhrl and Jürgen Barth not only brought this car across the line in seventh position overall, but also won the prize for the shortest time spent at the pits.

A further milestone in the history of Porsche's turbocharged competition cars was reached when

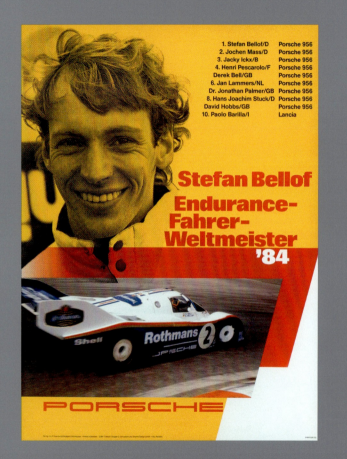

1. Stefan Bellof/D   Porsche 956
2. Jochen Mass/D   Porsche 956
3. Jacky Ickx/B   Porsche 956
4. Henri Pescarolo/F   Porsche 956
   Derek Bell/GB   Porsche 956
6. Jan Lammers/NL   Porsche 956
   Dr. Jonathan Palmer/GB Porsche 956
8. Hans Joachim Stuck/D   Porsche 956
   David Hobbs/GB   Porsche 956
10. Paolo Barilla/I   Lancia

Stefan Bellof

Endurance-Fahrer-Weltmeister '84

PORSCHE

Poster anlässlich des Gewinns der Lang-strecken-WM 1984
Poster announcing victory in the 1984 world long-distance championship

RECHTE SEITE: Presse-vorstellung des 962 C mit Doppelkupplungsgetriebe PDK auf dem Nürburgring (1987)
RIGHT PAGE: *Presenting the 962 C with PDK double clutch transmission to the media at the Nurburg Ring circuit (1987)*

Porsche 962 C LH
in Le Mans (1985)
*Porsche 962 C LH
in Le Mans, 1985*

sieg in Le Mans, sondern gewann zum Jahresende auch das Fahrer- und Marken-Championat. Im Rahmen der ständigen Verbesserungen mit einem elektronischen Einspritz- und Zündungssystem ausgestattet, war sein Sechszylinder-Turbo gleichermaßen leistungsstark wie sparsam. Im Renntempo bewegt, begnügte sich der bis zu 620 PS starke Boxermotor mit vergleichsweise geringen 50 Litern pro 100 Kilometer. Ab 1983 stand der 956 auch Privatteams zur Verfügung, so dass die Siegesserie nicht nur auf Werkswagen beschränkt blieb. Der Vorjahreserfolg wurde beim 24-Stunden-Rennen in Le Mans sogar noch übertroffen, als am Ende Porsche die Platzierungen Eins bis Acht belegte. Zum Saisonfinale verdichteten sich die zahlreichen Einzelsiege erneut zu internationalen Titeln, wie der Marken- und Langstreckenweltmeisterschaft. Einen einmaligen Rekord stellte dabei der 956-Pilot Stefan Bellof auf: Beim Training für das 1000-Kilometer-Rennen erzielte er erstmals in der Geschichte des Nürburgrings eine Durchschnittsgeschwindigkeit von mehr als 200 km/h.

Mit dem Typ 962 stellte Porsche 1985 eine nicht minder erfolgreiche Weiterentwicklung des 956 vor.

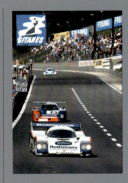

Porsche 962 C (Mass/Ickx) am 1. September 1985 in Spa
Porsche 962 C (Mass/Ickx) in Spa on September 1, 1985

the Type 956 was entered in Group C of the world long-distance racing championship. The first Porsche competition car with a monocoque, ground-effect chassis and body, it not only took the first three places at its first Le Mans appearance in 1982, but had made sure of both the drivers' and manufacturers' titles by the end of the season. With ongoing improvements, notably an electronic fuel injection and ignition system, its six-cylinder turbocharged engine was as economical as it was powerful. At race speeds, and although it developed up to 620 hp, the horizontally opposed engine consumed fuel at the comparatively low rate of 50 liters per 100 kilometers (4.7 US, 5.7 UK mpg). From 1983 on the 956 was also available to private teams that contributed even more to its run of victories. Even the previous year's one-two-three Le Mans success paled into insignificance when Porsche took the first eight places at the checkered flag. As the season drew to a close, the numerous individual wins coalesced into a string of international titles, including the manufacturers' and long-distance world championships. 956 driver Stefan Bellof set a unique record during practice for the 1000-kilometer race on Germany's Nurburg Ring when

Neben dem verlängerten Radstand und einem Stahl-Überrollkäfig wurde auch der Turbo-Motor modifiziert. Mit Luft-Wasserkühlung und bis zu 800 PS setzte der 962 die Porsche-Erfolge nicht nur in der Sportwagen-Weltmeisterschaft fort, sondern etablierte sich auch in der amerikanischen IMSA-Meisterschaft als Dauer-sieger. Mit insgesamt 51 Meisterschaftsteln und sieben Gesamtsiegen in Le Mans wurde der bis in die neunziger Jahre hinein eingesetzte Porsche 956/962 zum erfolgreichsten Rennsportwagen aller Zeiten.

Ein weiterer Höhepunkt in der Reihe der Porsche-Turbomotoren war der einmal mehr von Hans Mezger konstruierte »TAG-Turbo made by Porsche«. Der im Auftrag des britischen Rennstalls McLaren entwickelte und vom saudi-arabischen Geschäftsmann Mansour Ojjeh finanzierte Formel-1-Motor feierte im Sommer 1983 im McLaren MP4 seine Premiere. Als 1,5-Liter-Sechszylinder V-Motor mit Biturbo-Aufladung kon-struiert, leistete der ebenso leichte wie kompakte Antrieb bis zu 900 PS. Wichtige Neuheiten des Triebwerks waren unter anderem das elektronische Motormanagement, die Auslass-Sitzringkühlung oder die sphärische Anordnung der Ventile, was dem

he became the first driver to lap this racetrack at an average speed of more than 200 kph (124 mph).

The Porsche Type 962, introduced in 1985, was a development of the 956, and one that was to enjoy equal success. The wheelbase was lengthened, a steel roll cage installed and the turbocharged engine modified. With combined air and water cooling and a power output of up to 800 hp, the 962 not only continued Porsche's run of success in the world sports car championship but also began to collect wins one after another in the American IMSA series. The Porsche 956/962 continued to win races until the nineteen-nineties, and with 51 championship titles and seven overall victories in Le Mans, was the most successful sports racing car of all time.

Another highspot in the chronicle of Porsche's turbocharged engines was the "TAG-Turbo made by Porsche", another Hans Mezger design. Developed for the British McLaren racing team and financed by Saudi Arabian businessman Mansour Ojjeh, this Formula One engine was premiered in the McLaren MP4 in the summer of 1983. A V6 1.5-liter unit with

Motor insgesamt einen großen Technik-Vorsprung verschaffte. Mit 25 Grand-Prix-Siegen und drei WM-Titeln war der TAG-Turbo von 1984 bis 1986 das dominierende Triebwerk der Formel 1.

twin turbochargers, it was light in weight and compact in its overall dimensions, and could deliver a power output of up to 900 hp. Important new features included electronic engine management, exhaust valve seat cooling and a spherical valve layout. Together, these and other features put the engine well ahead in the technology race. With 25 Grand Prix wins and three world championship titles to its credit, the TAG Turbo dominated Formula One racing from 1984 to 1986.

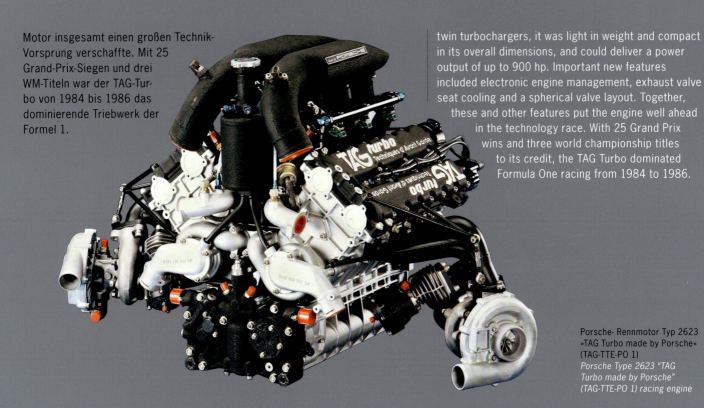

Porsche- Rennmotor Typ 2623 »TAG Turbo made by Porsche« (TAG-TTE-PO 1)
Porsche Type 2623 "TAG Turbo made by Porsche" (TAG-TTE-PO 1) racing engine

Rollout des McLaren Formel 1 mit Porsche-Turbomotor auf der Teststrecke in Weissach (1983)
Rollout for the McLaren Formula One car with Porsche turbocharged engine on the test track in Weissach (1983)

RECHTE SEITE: Der 1988 für die amerikanische CART-Serie entwickelte Typ 2708 war eine Neuentwicklung mit Aluminium-Kunstoff-Monocoque. Als Antrieb diente ein V8-Turbo mit 750 PS

RIGHT PAGE: *Developed in 1988 for the American CART race series, the Type 2708 was an entirely new design with an aluminium and plastic monocoque body, powered by a turbocharged 750-hp V8 engine*

DER URKNALL – PORSCHE 911 TURBO 3.0
THE BIG BANG – PORSCHE 911 TURBO 3.0

DER URKNALL – PORSCHE 911 TURBO 3.0
THE BIG BANG – PORSCHE 911 TURBO 3.0

Im September 1973 stand auf der Frankfurter IAA ein silbernes 911-Coupé, das den Puls der anwesenden Automobil-Liebhaber bereits im Stand in die Höhe trieb. Optisch erinnerte das Messefahrzeug an einen 911 Carrera RS 3.0, doch machten große Schriftzüge auf den hinteren Kotflügeln deutlich, dass es sich um ein völlig neues Modell handelte: »Turbo« hieß das Zauberwort, welches die Sportwagenwelt elektrisierte. Mit genauen Informationen über den Wagen wurde zwar gegeizt, aber die Porsche-Pressesprecher ließen durchblicken, dass es sich um den Prototypen einer geplanten Turbo-Version des 911 handle.

Ein Jahr darauf, im Oktober 1974, wurde die serienreife Variante des 911 Turbo auf dem Pariser Automobilsalon vorgestellt. Mit dieser »Krönung einer

Premiere des 911 Turbo auf der IAA 1973
Premiere for the 911 Turbo at the 1973 German Motor Show

LINKE SEITE: Ur-Typ des Porsche 911 Turbo 3.0 (1973)
LEFT PAGE: *The first-ever Porsche 911 Turbo 3.0 (1973)*

It's September 1973, and visitors to the German "IAA" Motor Show in Frankfurt can see a silver-painted 911 Coupe that puts up their pulse rates even when viewed at a standstill. The show car looks very similar to a 911 Carrera RS 3.0, but bold lettering on the rear fenders tells the world that it's a totally new model. "Turbo" is the magic word that causes a tremor of anticipation to run through the sports-car world. Precise information on the new model is sparse, but Porsche's press officers were at least prepared to say that it was the prototype of a planned version of the 911 with a turbocharged engine.

A year later, in October 1974, the series-production version of the 911 Turbo was premiered at the Paris Motor Show. This "culmination of a well-proven design",

bewährten Konstruktion« stieß der kleine Zuffenhausener Sportwagenhersteller in das oberste aller Marktsegmente vor. Als weltweit erster Seriensportwagen mit abgasseitig geregeltem Turbolader war der Porsche 911 Turbo eines der schnellsten Automobile seiner Zeit und spielte mit 65.800 DM auch preislich in der Liga der Supersportwagen mit. Sein Grundpreis zeugte von großen Selbstbewusstsein, denn er übertraf sogar den neuen Ferrari 308 GT4 um fast 17.000 DM. Doch im Gegensatz zu seinen exotischen Konkurrenten war der 911 Turbo ein voll alltagstauglicher Luxus-Sportwagen und wurde von Porsche auch als solcher positioniert. In der Pressemitteilung vom September 1974 betonte Porsche die »kultivierte Kraft« und »exklusive Sportlichkeit« des 260 PS starken Modells, das sich neben technischen Leckerbissen, wie dem ladedruckgesteuerten Abgas-Turbolader oder den innenbelüfteten Scheibenbremsen, durch eine besonders exquisite Innenausstattung auszeichnete.

Serienmäßig wurde der Fahrer unter anderem durch ein Dreispeichen-Lederlenkrad, Scheinwerfer-Reinigungsanlage, Stereo-Radio, elektrische

Verleiht Flügel: Porsche 911 Turbo (Modelljahr 1975)
Takes wing: Porsche 911 Turbo (1975 model year)

as the critics have it, took the small Zuffenhausen-based sports car manufacturer into the highest market segment of all. The first sports car in the world to have a turbocharger regulated on the exhaust side of the engine, the Porsche 911 Turbo was one of the fastest cars of its time. Its selling price of 65,800 Deutschmarks (DM) put it squarely in the supersport category: the Ferrari 308 GT4, also new at that time, cost almost 17,000 DM less. To a greater extent than this exotic competitor, however, the 911 Turbo was a luxury sports car entirely suitable for day-to-day driving. This was the positioning that Porsche chose for it. The press release in September 1974 emphasized the "cultured power" and "exclusive sporting character" of the new model, which had a 260-hp engine, many fascinating new technical features such as exhaust-side control of the turbocharger and ventilated brake disks, but also specially selected, luxurious interior equipment and trim.

The driver enjoyed both luxury and efficiency: the car's specification included a leather-covered three-spoke steering wheel, a headlamp cleaning system, stereo radio, electric window lifts, automatic heating

Die Markteinführung des
911 Turbo erfolgte 1974
*The 911 Turbo had its
market launch in 1974*

Fensterheber, automatisch geregelte Heizung und eine Ganzlederausstattung verwöhnt. Optisch machte der 911 Turbo durch seinen dominanten Heckflügel, eine PU-Frontspoilerlippe und breite Kotflügel im Stil eines Carrera RSR auf sich aufmerksam, unter denen vorne 185er und hinten 215er Breitreifen auf 15-Zoll Fuchs-Felgen rollten. Eine kleine stilistische Revolution wagten die Porsche-Designer, indem sie beim 911 Turbo auf jeglichen Zierat aus Chrom verzichteten: Selbst die Lampenringe und der Rückspiegel waren in mattem Schwarz gehalten, und auch auf dem Heck wies ein schwarzer Schriftzug auf die potente Motorisierung hin.

Technisch brachte der intern Typ 930 genannte Sportwagen viele Details aus dem Rennwagenbau auf die Straße. So stammte die Kinematik der Vorder- und Hinterachse vom RSR, die steifen Radträger vom 917. Die ursprüngliche Heimat der kontaktlosen Batterie-Hochleistungs-Kondensator-Zündung (BHKZ) sowie der in Reihe geschalteten Kraftstoffpumpen war ebenfalls die Rennstrecke. Von den üblichen 911-Saugmotoren unterschied sich der auf 3 Liter Hubraum vergrößerte Turbo-Antrieb Typ 930/50 erheblich: Neben einem

LINKE SEITE: Exklusive Sportlichkeit im 911 Turbo (Modelljahr 1977)
LEFT PAGE: *Sporting style and exclusive character in the 911 Turbo (1977 model year)*

Der 3-Liter-Motor des Porsche 911 Turbo (1975)
The Porsche 911 Turbo's 3-liter engine (1975)

control and full leather upholstery and trim. Visual evidence of the 911 Turbo was the dominant rear wing, a plastic (PU) front spoiler lip and flared fenders in the same style as the Carrera RSR. Equally eye-catching: the size 185 front and 215 rear tires on 15-inch Fuchs wheels. Porsche's designers decided to risk a minor styling revolution on the 911 Turbo by leaving off all the usual chrome trim. Even the headlamp rims and outside mirrors had a matt black paint finish, and the lettering at the rear that identified this most potent of Porsche models was also in black.

Known internally as the Type 930, the new sports car featured many technical details taken directly from motor sport. The front and rear suspension layouts were from the RSR, the extremely rigid wheel hub assemblies from the 917. The contactless high-performance battery and capacitor ignition (BHKZ) and the in-series fuel pumps were also sourced from competition practice. The Type 930/50 turbocharged engine, with its capacity increased to 3 liters, was considerably different from the naturally aspirated units in the other 911 models: as well as a light alloy crankcase, Nikasil coated cylinder walls, a

Leichtmetall-Kurbelgehäuse, Nikasil-beschichteten Zylindern, einer größeren Kupplung und einem zusätzlichen Ölkühler verbauten die Porsche-Ingenieure ein neues Viergang-Getriebe (Typ 930/30), das sich den 343 Newtonmetern Drehmoment gewachsen zeigte. Gegenüber der normalen 911-Schaltbox (Typ 915) waren für das Turbo-Getriebe Wellen, Lager, Radsätze und Achsantrieb wesentlich verstärkt worden. Aufgrund der breiten Gangräder und des vergrößerten Tellerraddurchmessers konnte angesichts der beengten Platzverhältnisse nur ein Viergang-Getriebe verwirklicht werden, was die Ingenieure aufgrund des hohen Motordrehmoments als völlig ausreichend ansahen. Und auch das Thema Umwelt spielte bei der Entwicklung des Serien-Turbo von Anfang an eine Rolle. Durch seine einzigartige Kombination aus Abgasturboaufladung und kontinuierlicher Benzineinspritzung, der Bosch K-Jetronic, konnte der 911 Turbo von Beginn an die strengen amerikanischen Abgasvorschriften erfüllen.

Die Fahrleistungen des »Über-Porsche« lagen 1974 im Grenzbereich der Vorstellungskraft. Von 0 auf 100 km/h ermittelte die Automobilzeitschrift »auto,

Getriebe Typ 930/30
Type 930/30 gearbox

larger clutch and an additional oil cooler, Porsche's engineers had developed a new four-speed gearbox (Type 930/30) capable of withstanding the engine's peak torque of 343 Newton-meters. Compared with the regular gearbox (Type 915), the shafts, bearings, gear sets and output shaft were all uprated for much greater strength. The wider gearwheels and increased crown wheel diameter occupied more space, so that only a four-speed gearbox was practicable, but in view of the high engine torque Porsche's engineers were convinced that four gears would be enough. Protection of the environment was also given close attention when the production Turbo was developed: thanks to the unique combination of turbocharging and Bosch K-Jetronic continuous fuel injection, the 911 Turbo was able to comply from the start with the tough American exhaust emission limits.

Back in 1974, hardly anyone had encountered a sports car like this "Super-Porsche" or could visualize how it performed. The German car magazine "auto, motor und sport" timed the Turbo from a standing start to 100 kph (62 mph) in 5.5 seconds, more than a second faster than comparable rivals. The top speed was

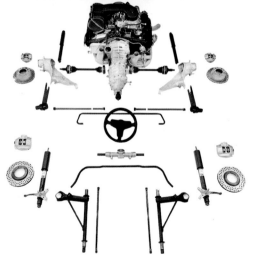

Vom Rennsport in die Serie:
911 Turbo (links) und 911
Carrera RSR Turbo 2.1
From motor racing
to series production:
911 Turbo (left) and
911 Carrera RSR Turbo 2.1

motor und sport« einen Wert, der fast eine Sekunde schneller als vergleichbare Mitbewerber war: 5,5 Sekunden. Als Höchstgeschwindigkeit wurden »über 250 km/h« bei 6.000/min erreicht, was 1974 auch den Durchschnittsverbrauch von 20,9 Liter als moderat erscheinen ließ. Doch beim Fahrverhalten mahnten die Tester zu erhöhter Aufmerksamkeit und rieten künftigen Turbo-Fahrern angesichts der explosiven Kraftentfaltung des Turbo-Triebwerks zur »Mark Donohue-Fahrweise«: Langsam in die Kurve hineinfahren und dafür früh mit Vollgas hinaus beschleunigen.

Zügig bewegt, war beim 911 Turbo der ersten Generation stets ein erhöhtes Maß an Aufmerksamkeit angebracht. Turbo-Piloten, die sich überschätzten oder bei Nässe unvorsichtig waren, wurden nur zu häufig von der explosiven Kraftentfaltung des Motors überrascht. Schnell hatte der 911 Turbo den Ruf weg, ein Sportwagen für echte Männer zu sein. Vielleicht gerade deswegen zählten auch viele Damen zum exklusiven Kreis der Turbo-Kunden. Allen voran Louise Piëch, die 1974 von ihrem Bruder Ferry Porsche den allerersten 911 Turbo zum Geburtstag erhielt.

Die Nr. 1 des 911 Turbo wurde von Louise Piëch gefahren
The first 911 Turbo to be built was driven by Louise Piëch

LINKE SEITE: An der Spitze des Porsche-Modellprogramms 1977: der 911 Turbo
LEFT PAGE: *Spearheading the 1977 Porsche model program: the 911 Turbo*

quoted as "over 250 kph" (155 mph) at an engine speed of 6000 rpm. In 1974 an average fuel consumption of 20.9 liters per 100 kilometers (11.1 US, 13.5 UK mpg) still seemed fairly moderate. But in view of this performance, road testers warned readers who might be planning to buy the Turbo to exercise special care. Its explosive power delivery, they implied, called for a "Mark Donohue" driving style: slowly into corners, with full power only applied when returning to a straight line. It's certainly true that Turbo drivers who overestimated their own skills or were careless in wet weather could be taken unawares by the way the power came in. The 911 Turbo soon acquired the reputation that only "real men" could handle it. Possibly as a reaction to this prejudice, many women were also to be found among the exclusive group of Turbo drivers, notably Louise Piëch, who received the very first 911 Turbo from her brother Ferry Porsche as a birthday present in 1974.

Porsche's "road turbo" was partly a response to the activities of Bavarian carmaker BMW, which exhibited a design study in 1972 with gull-wing doors and a turbocharged engine, and followed this up from

Mit dem »Straßenturbo« reagierte Porsche nicht zuletzt auf die Aktivitäten des bayerischen Autobauers BMW, der 1972 die Studie eines Turbo-Flügeltürers vorgestellt hatte und ab August 1973 eine Turbo-Version der Limousine 2002 anbot. Doch während der durch Ölkrise und Motorprobleme gebeutelte BMW 2002 turbo nach etwas über einem Jahr wieder eingestellt wurde, startete Porsche erst durch. Auf dem Höhepunkt der schwersten Rezession der Nachkriegszeit wagte der Stuttgarter Sportwagenspezialist die Flucht nach vorne und präsentierte im Herbst 1974 ein neues Spitzenmodell, das alles Bisherige in den Schatten stellte. Nach der Einführung des 911 Turbo herrschte in Zuffenhausen erst einmal banges Warten, ob sich das teure Topmodell in ausreichender Stückzahl verkaufen ließe. Der Ölboykott der OPEC hatte auf dem Automobilmarkt Spuren hinterlassen und die Erinnerungen an Tempolimits und Sonntagsfahrverbote waren Ende 1974 noch frisch. Damit der 911 Turbo als Rennsportbasis genutzt werden konnte, mussten gemäß dem Gruppe-4-Reglement immerhin 400 Autos gebaut werden. Den Gedanken, es bei einer Kleinserie zu belassen, wischte der Porsche-Vorstand Heinz Branitzki selbstbewusst vom Tisch: »Wenn wir nicht in der Lage sind, ein so

Modelljahr 1976:
Porsche 911 Turbo (vorne);
Porsche 911 2,7 (orange);
Porsche 911 Carrera 3.0
Targa (rechts)
1976 model year:
Porsche 911 Turbo (front);
Porsche 911 2.7 (orange)
and Porsche 911 Carrera
3.0 Targa (right)

RECHTE SEITE: Meerblick:
Porsche 911 Turbo 3.0
(Modelljahr 1976)
RIGHT PAGE: *Glimpse of the*
sea: Porsche 911 Turbo 3.0
(1976 model year)

August 1973 on with a turbocharged version of its 2002 sedan. This model appeared at an ill-chosen moment during an international oil crisis, and also suffered from engine problems; it went out of production after rather more than a year. Porsche, on the other hand, chose attack as the best form of defense. In the fall of 1974, at the peak of the worst recession since the end of the war, Porsche launched a new top model that outclassed everything that had come before in this market segment. Having introduced the 911 Turbo, the management in Zuffenhausen had to endure a nail-biting period of waiting to see whether the car would sell in sufficient numbers to pay for itself. The OPEC oil boycott had seriously affected the car market, and even at the end of 1974 the German driver was only too well aware of the speed limits and bans on Sunday driving that had been imposed. At least 400 cars had to be built before the 911 Turbo could be homologated as a Group 4 competition car. Some company executives were of the opinion that a short production run would be sufficient, but Porsche director Heinz Branitzki was confident: "If we're not capable of selling such a superb product as this, then it's time for us to

großartiges Produkt zu verkaufen, dann ist es an der Zeit für uns, aus dem Sportwagenbau auszusteigen.« Als die Produktion des 911 Turbo im März 1975 anlief, war der neue Porsche durch zahlreiche Testberichte der internationalen Automagazine bereits in aller Munde. Die Tester waren beeindruckt von der einmaligen Leistungscharakteristik des 911 Turbo und gaben ihre Begeisterung an die Leser weiter. Die deutsche »auto, motor und sport« attestierte ihm »Dampf in allen Gassen« und eine »völlig neue Dimension der Kraftentfaltung«. Die britische »Autocar« bezeichnete den Turbo als »Ausnahme-Auto« und »Motor« wählte ihn zum besten Sportwagen des Jahres 1975 und zur »besten Fahrmaschine, die es für Geld zu kaufen gibt.« Selbst im Heimatland des 55-Meilen-Speedlimits, den USA, wurde der ab dem Modelljahr 1976 ausgelieferte 911 Turbo Carrera, so die dortige Verkaufsbezeichnung, begeistert empfangen. Für die amerikanischen Kunden hatte Porsche eigens eine besondere, abgasentgiftete Version entwickelt, um die strengen Gesetze zur Luftreinhaltung einzuhalten. Die Export-Motoren wurden mit einer Zusatzlufteinblasung, mit Abgasrückführung ins Ansaugsystem (EGR) sowie mit einem der Turbine vorgeschalteten Thermoreaktor ausgestattet, so dass

US-Werbeanzeige für den 911 Turbo Carrera (1976)
US advertising for the 911 Turbo Carrera (1976)

LINKE SEITE: Die US-Version hieß 911 Turbo Carrera
LEFT PAGE: *The US version was known as the 911 Turbo Carrera*

give up building sports cars altogether!" When production of the 911 Turbo started in March 1975, the new Porsche was already the subject of keen public interest, thanks to a number of test reports in car magazines. The testers were impressed by the 911 Turbo's unique performance, and didn't hesitate to pass this enthusiasm on to their readers. The German car magazine "auto, motor und sport" declared that "it builds up a tremendous head of steam" and that "its power flow is in an entirely new dimension". For the British magazine "Autocar", the Turbo was an "altogether exceptional car". In 1975, "Motor" voted it best sports car of the year and described it as "the best driving machine that money can buy". Even in the USA, a country with a 55 mph speed limit imposed almost everywhere, the 911 Turbo Carrera as it was known there was given an overwhelmingly enthusiastic reception when deliveries started in the 1976 model year. For its American customers, Porsche developed a special version with full exhaust emission control to comply with tough air pollution laws. If cars were exported, their engines had additional air injection, exhaust gas recirculation (EGR) and a thermo-reactor ahead of the

der Turbo-Porsche neben dem US-Markt auch in Kanada und Japan zugelassen werden konnte.

Ein Jahr nach Produktionsbeginn stand fest, dass sich der 911 Turbo zu einem echten Verkaufserfolg entwickelt hatte. Im Mai 1976 wurde in Zuffenhausen in einer Zeremonie der 1000. Turbo gefeiert und an seine Besitzerin, die Prinzessin Antoinette zu Fürstenberg, übergeben. Viele andere Prominente begeisterten sich ebenfalls für das »It car« aus Stuttgart-Zuffenhausen. Zu den Turbo-Fahrern der ersten Stunde zählten beispielsweise Künstler wie der Dirigent Herbert von Karajan, Sportler wie Fussball-Star Uli Hoeneß oder Unternehmer wie der Verleger Paul Pietsch. Der Ur-Turbo wurde zu einem Erfolgstyp, von dem allein während der ersten drei Modelljahre 2.850 Einheiten produziert wurden.

Übergabe des 1000. Turbo an Prinzessin Antoinette zu Fürstenberg
Handing over the 1000th Turbo to Princess Antoinette zu Fürstenberg

turbocharger turbine. These modifications enabled the Porsche Turbo to be sold in Canada and Japan as well as in the USA.

After a year's production, it was clear to everyone concerned that the 911 Turbo was a genuine sales success. A ceremony was held at the Zuffenhausen plant in May 1976 to mark the production of the 1,000th Turbo, which was handed over to its owner, Princess Antoinette zu Fürstenberg. Many other prominent personalities were unable to resist Porsche's "in" car. Among the first to take delivery were artists such as the celebrated conductor Herbert von Karajan, sport stars like soccer player Uli Hoeness and businessmen like publisher Paul Pietsch. The first-ever Porsche Turbo had proved to be a best-seller, with 2,850 built in the first three model years alone.

Freizeitvergnügen:
Porsche 911 Turbo 3,0
(Modelljahr 1977)
Leisure and pleasure:
Porsche 911 Turbo 3.0
(1977 model year)

DER DAUERLÄUFER: PORSCHE 911 TURBO 3.3
LONG-DISTANCE RUNNER: THE PORSCHE 911 TURBO 3.3

DER DAUERLÄUFER: PORSCHE 911 TURBO 3.3
LONG-DISTANCE RUNNER: THE PORSCHE 911 TURBO 3.3

Eines der Erfolgsgeheimnisse der Baureihe 911 war die ständige und konsequente technische Weiterentwicklung. Jedes Jahr wurde der Elfer in vielen Details verbessert, so dass er Ferry Porsches Ideal vom perfekten Sportwagen immer näher kam. Diese Philosophie wurde auch beim 911 Turbo angewandt. Ab dem Modelljahr 1977 werteten etwa eine Ladedruckanzeige, 16-Zoll-Felgen oder ein Bremskraftverstärker den teuersten aller Serien-Porsche auf.

Nach nur drei Jahren Bauzeit folgte dann eine umfassende Überarbeitung, die den Leistungsvorsprung des Turbo auf Jahre hinaus sichern sollte. Die zum Modelljahr 1978 eingeführte, zweite Generation des 911 Turbo mit dem berühmten 3,3-Liter-Triebwerk wurde bis ins Jahr 1989 produziert – ein Zeitraum, der angesichts der Dauer heutiger Produktzyklen staunen lässt.

LINKE SEITE: Generationswechsel: Porsche 911 Turbo 3.3 (Modelljahr 1978)
LEFT PAGE: *Generation change: Porsche 911 Turbo 3.3 (1978 model year)*

Der 3,3-Liter-Motor mit Abgasturbolader und Ladeluftkühler
3.3-liter engine with turbocharger and charge-air intercooler

One of the Porsche 911 model line's success secrets has been its systematic, unceasing technical development. Every year, a number of design details were improved to bring the car closer to Ferry Porsche's ideal of the perfect sports car. The same policy was applied to the 911 Turbo. In the 1977 model year, for instance, this most expensive of all series-production Porsches was upgraded with a boost pressure display, 16-inch wheels and a brake booster servo.

After only three years in production, it underwent an extensive design revision, the aim being to give it sufficient performance to maintain its market lead for a number of years to come. Introduced in the 1978 model year, the second-generation Turbo had the celebrated 3.3-liter engine, and remained in production until 1989 – an almost unbelievably long model life-cycle compared with modern practice in the automobile industry.

Die weitreichende Überarbeitung des Turbo-Trieb-werks der so genannten »L-Serie« des 911 ging zum einen auf die strengen Umweltanforderungen einiger Märkte zurück, zum anderen war es eine Reaktion auf den 1977 eingeführten Porsche 928. Mit 240 PS und einem Grundpreis von fast 60.000 DM kam der 928 dem 911 Turbo in puncto Leistung und Exklusivität recht nahe, weshalb Porsche den Respektabstand des Topmodells wieder herstellen wollte. Hauptmerkmale des überarbeiteten 911 Turbo waren eine Hubraum-erweiterung auf 3,3 Liter sowie ein Ladeluftkühler, der unterhalb des Heckspoilers positioniert wurde. Aus dem Rennsport abgeleitet, war dieser eine Weltneu-heit beim Bau von Serien-Pkw. Der Ladeluftkühler verringerte die Ansaugtemperatur der Luft um bis zu 100 Grad Celsius, wodurch der Motor mehr Leistung und Drehmoment in allen Drehzahlbereichen erzielte. Das Resultat waren standfeste 300 PS bei 5.500 /min und ein maximales Drehmoment von 412 Newtonmetern.

Der aktiven Fahrsicherheit des 911 Turbo 3.3 kam eine neue, selbst entwickelte Leichtmetall-Brems-anlage zugute. Mit dieser nutzte Porsche einmal mehr die in Langstreckenrennen gesammelten Erfahrungen,

Rennerprobt: Die Brems-anlage des 911 Turbo 3.3 stammt vom Porsche 917
Race-tested: the 911 Turbo 3.3's brakes came from the Porsche 917

The »L« series turbocharged engine for the 911 was revised because environmental protection demands in certain markets were becoming more and more difficult to satisfy, but also as a reaction to the Porsche 928, introduced in 1977. With a power output of 240 hp and a list price of under 60,000 Deutschmarks (DM), the 928 was very close to the 911 Turbo in both performance and exclusive character, and Porsche therefore wanted to move its top model higher up the scale to avoid any internal marketing conflict. The main features of the latest 911 Turbo were an increase in engine size to 3.3 liters and a charge-air intercooler located under the rear spoiler. This device, adopted from the motor racing scene, had never before been used anywhere in the world on a production car. The intercooler lowered the intake air temperature by as much as 100 degrees Centigrade. This cold air of increased density improved cylinder filling and enabled the engine to develop more power and torque over the entire speed range. The new Turbo demonstrated this with a reliable 300 horsepower at 5,500 revolutions a minute, and a maximum torque of 412 Newton-meters.

Der ladeluftgekühlte 3,3-
Liter-Motor leistete 300 PS
*With charge-air intercooling,
the 3.3-liter engine
developed 300 hp*

Von 0–100 km/h
beschleunigte der Turbo 3.3
in 5,4 Sekunden
*The Turbo 3.3 accelerated
from 0 to 100 kph (62 mph)
in 5.4 seconds*

was angesichts der Höchstgeschwindigkeit von 260 km/h beruhigend war. Die Vierkolben-Festsattelbremse mit gelochten, innenbelüfteten Bremsscheiben entstammte dem Porsche 917, der einige Jahre zuvor die Rennstrecken der Welt dominiert hatte.

Optisch blieben die Unterschiede zum Vorgängermodell moderat. Auffälligstes Merkmal des 911 Turbo 3.3 war sein von einem PU-Schaumrand (im Porsche-Jargon »Gummi-Lippe« genannt) eingefasster Heckspoiler, im Innenraum wies ein 300 Kilometer-Tacho auf das Leistungspotenzial des schnellsten aller Serien-Porsche hin. Doch nicht nur die Leistung, auch der Preis des Spitzenmodells war erhöht worden: Mit 78.500 DM war der neue Turbo zwar kein Schnäppchen, doch kostete ein bei den Fahrleistungen ebenbürtiger Lamborghini Countach noch einmal 50.000 DM mehr.

Das solide technische Gesamtpaket sollte der 911 Turbo 3.3 über viele Jahre behalten und es sollte dabei ständig weiter optimiert werden. Im Zuge dieser kontinuierlichen Modellpflege gelang den Porsche-Ingenieuren 1982 ein großer Schritt: Durch eine

For even greater road safety, the 911 Turbo 3.3 had new light alloy brakes developed by Porsche's own engineers. Once again, they were able to make use of the accumulated know-how from many long-distance races – a comforting thought in view of the car's top speed of 260 kph (162 mph). The four-piston fixed caliper brakes with perforated and internally ventilated disks were based on those fitted to the Porsche 917, the competition car that had dominated the world's racetracks a few years earlier.

There were only a few changes in appearance compared with the previous model. The 911 Turbo 3.3's most striking visual feature was the rear spoiler with its foamed polyurethane border (known disrespectfully in Porsche jargon as the "rubber lip"). Inside the car, a 300 kph (190 mph) tacho dial was a subtle reminder of the performance potential available from the fastest of all production Porsches. Together with this performance hike, the price had to be slightly increased: at 78,500 Deutschmarks (DM), the Turbo was certainly not a cut-price offer, but a Lamborghini Countach delivering equivalent performance cost 50,000 DM more.

US-Werbeanzeige
(1977)
*Advertising for the
US model, 1977*

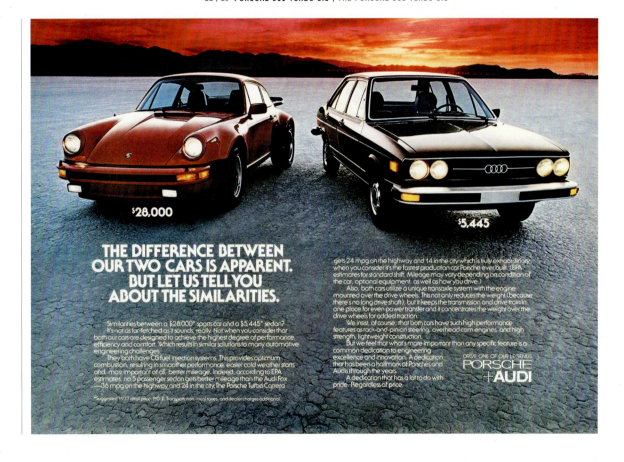

Goldene Zeiten: Porsche
911 Turbo 3.3 (Modelljahr
1983)
*Golden age: Porsche 911
Turbo 3.3 (1983 model
year)*

gründliche Überarbeitung der Gemischaufbereitung sank der Verbrauch trotz unveränderter Leistung deutlich. Statt mit 20 Litern kam man jetzt mit 15,5 Litern durch den Stadtverkehr, bei Tempo 120 begnügte sich der Turbo jetzt mit 11,8 statt bisher 15,3 Litern. Gemäß der Porsche-Philosophie von der »schrittweisen Evolution« erhielt der 911 Turbo 3.3 bald darauf einen neuen Kettenspanner mit Drucköschmierung, im modifizierten Innenraum sorgten dezentere Farben und Stoffe für ein zeitgemäßes Ambiente.

Auf den Ende der siebziger Jahre entstehenden Trend der Fahrzeug-Individualisierung reagierte Porsche mit einem umfangreichen Sonderwunschprogramm, das automobile Träume Realität werden ließ. Ab dem Modelljahr 1983 konnte die Turbo-Karosserie in einer optisch vom Rennwagentyp 935 abgeleiteten »Flachbau«-Variante mit Klappscheinwerfern geordert werden. Gerne mit aerodynamischen Schwellerverkleidungen und Zusatzlufteinlässen an den hinteren Kotflügeln kombiniert, wurden die in der Szene »Flachschnauzer« genannten 911 Turbo zu einer Zeitgeist-Ikone der achtziger Jahre. Neben dem Aerodynamik-Paket

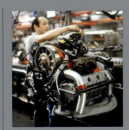

Montage des 3,3-Liter Turbomotors
Assembling the 3.3-liter turbocharged engine

The 911 Turbo 3.3 was a mature technical package in every respect, and remained unchanged apart from regular detail optimization for a number of years. This was the situation until 1982, when Porsche's engineers took another big step forward: the mixture preparation system was thoroughly revised and as a result fuel consumption went down significantly with no loss of power. The test-cycle figure in urban traffic improved from 20 to 15.5 liters per 100 km (15.2 US, 18.2 UK mpg) and at 120 kph (75 mph), the Turbo was now content with 11.8 l/100 km (19.9 US, 23.9 UK mpg) instead of the previous 15.3 l/100 km. In accordance with Porsche's policy of step-by-step evolution, the 911 Turbo 3.3 was next given a new chain tensioner with pressurized oil lubrication; the car's interior was redesigned with restrained colors and materials, for a more modern ambiente.

At the end of the nineteen-seventies a strong trend toward customization of production cars to suit the individual owner's personality grew up. Porsche responded with an extensive program of optional extras aimed at making dream cars come true. Starting in the 1983 model year, a special lowered

Sonderwunschprogramm:
911 Turbo 3.3 Flachbau
(Modelljahr 1983)
With optional extras:
911 Turbo 3.3 with lowered
body (1983 model year)

kümmerte sich die Porsche-Reparaturabteilung auf Wunsch auch um den Turbo-Antrieb, für den werksseitig eine Leistungssteigerung angeboten wurde. Durch die Verwendung eines größeren Turboladers mit optimiertem Ladeluftkühler und einer Sport-Auspuffanlage stieg die Motorleistung auf 330 PS. Ein solcher werksgetunter 911 Turbo 3.3 beschleunigte in 5,2 Sekunden auf 100 km/h und erreichte in der Flachbau-Variante bis zu 275 Stundenkilometer. Nicht nur bei der Endgeschwindigkeit, auch beim Preis stieß Porsche mit diesen Supersportwagen in neue Regionen vor. Für einen kompletten Umbau mussten Mitte der achtziger Jahre bis zu 200.000 DM investiert werden, was aber 948 Kunden nicht daran hinderte, sich ihren Traum vom individuellen Porsche 911 Turbo zu verwirklichen.

Als besondere Spezialität für sonnen- und leistungshungrige Kunden präsentierte Porsche im Frühjahr 1987 das erste 911 Turbo Cabriolet. Zusammen mit dem 911 Turbo Targa bildete das 300 PS starke und 147.850 DM teure Cabriolet die Speerspitze im Porsche-Verkaufsprogramm. Neben den außergewöhnlichen Fahrleistungen zeigte sich die Fachpresse besonders von der Karosseriesteifigkeit beeindruckt,

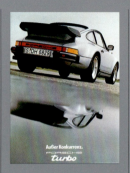

Werbeplakat (1977)
Advertising poster, 1977

version of the Turbo body with pop-up headlamps, based visually on the 935 race car, was introduced. Most customers liked to combine this with aerodynamically effective sill trims and additional air inlets in the rear fenders. The 911 Turbo "Flatnose", as it was nicknamed, soon became a cult car of the nineteen-eighties. As well as the aerodynamic package, Porsche's workshop was prepared as a further option to tweak the turbocharged engine and boost its power output. The size of the turbocharger was increased, and together with an optimized charge-air intercooler and a sport exhaust system boosted power output to 330 hp. With this degree of factory tuning, the 911 Turbo 3.3 could reach 100 kph (62 mph) from a standing start in 5.2 seconds; the top speed of the lowered-body version went up to 275 kilometers an hour (171 mph). These impressive figures were felt to justify a price increase that took Porsche's supersport model into new realms: for the complete conversion, up to 200,000 DM were charged in the mid-eighties, but this outlay didn't deter 948 customers from fulfilling their dream of the ultimate creation, an individually configured Porsche 911 Turbo.

denn im Gegensatz zu den meisten zeitgenössischen Cabriolets waren für den offenen Elfer Verwindungsgeräusche der Karosserie ein Fremdwort. Die anspruchsvollen Kunden wurden im 911 Turbo Cabriolet nicht nur durch Leistung, sondern auch durch Luxus verwöhnt: Neben den serienmäßig voll-elektrischen Sitzen, Lederausstattung, Klimaanlage und Zentralverriegelung war als Sonderwunsch auch ein elektrisches Verdeck ohne Aufpreis orderbar.

Mitte der achtziger Jahre wurde der weltweite Trend zu Abgas-Katalysatoren zu einer echten Herausforderung für die Motorenentwickler der Turbo-Baureihe. Die strengen Abgasvorschriften in Nordamerika führten dazu, dass Porsche den 911 Turbo 1984 nicht mehr in die USA exportieren konnte, da das Triebwerk nicht für eine Katalysatortechnik ausgelegt war. Alternativ war zwar der 911 Carrera im »Turbo-Look« erhältlich, doch war dies keine wünschenswerte Alternative für das renditestarke Topmodell. Unterdessen wurde unter Hochdruck an dem vom Porsche 959 abgeleiteten Typ 965 gearbeitet, der im obersten Marktsegment den Turbo 3.3 ersetzen sollte. Mit 360 PS-Biturbo und digitalem Motormanagement sollte

Offenes Vergnügen: Ab 1987 war der 911 Turbo 3.3 auch als Cabriolet und Targa erhältlich
Open for pleasure: from 1987 on, the 911 Turbo 3.3 was also available in Convertible and Targa body styles

Porsche announced a special treat for sun- and performance-loving customers in the spring of 1978: the first 911 Turbo Convertible. Together with the 911 Turbo Targa, this model, which had a 300-hp engine and cost 147,850 DM, formed the spearhead of the Porsche sales offensive. As well as the unusually high performance, the car journalists were full of praise for the rigidity of the body: unlike many convertibles being produced at that time, the open-top 911 was free from structural distortion and the associated noise. Customers with demanding standards not only found in the 911 Turbo Convertible the performance they were seeking, but also a high standard of luxury: seats with full electric adjustment, leather upholstery and trim, air conditioning and central locking. As an option, the soft top could be raised and lowered electrically at no extra charge.

In the early nineteen-eighties, the automobile industry began to adopt the catalytic converter for exhaust emission control. This presented Porsche's engine developers with a considerable challenge: Stringent North American anti-pollution laws meant that Porsche was unable to export the 911 Turbo to the USA in

Leserwahl '83
auto motor sport
DIE BESTEN AUTOS DER WELT

Porsche 911 Turbo:
„Bester Sportwagen der Welt"

S·ET 9392

PORSCHE
FAHREN IN SEINER SCHÖNSTEN FORM.

Werbeplakat (1983)
Advertising poster, 1983

RECHTE SEITE:
Werbeanzeige aus dem Jahr 1985
RIGHT PAGE: *Advertisement dating from 1985*

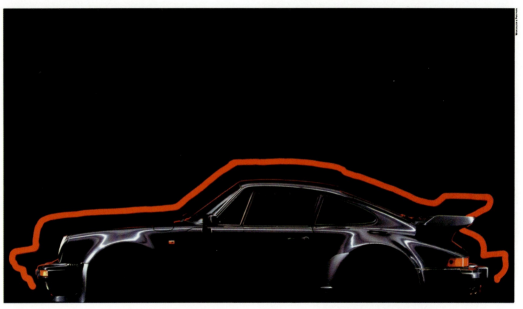

der 965 auch den strengsten Umweltanforderungen gerecht werden, doch das Projekt wurde 1989 aus modellpolitischen Gründen gestoppt. Vor die Wahl gestellt, den wichtigen US-Markt für den 911 Turbo zu verlieren oder eine Leistungseinbuße in Kauf zu nehmen, entwickelten die Ingenieure 1985 eine »entgiftete« Export-Version mit modifizierter Gemischaufbereitung, 3-Wege-Katalysator, Lambdasonde und Sekundärlufteinblasung. Trotz dieser Maßnahmen leistete der für bleifreies Benzin ausgelegte US-Motor noch 285 PS.

Ende 1988 löste Porsche einen lang gehegten Wunsch vieler Turbo Kunden ein. Nach 14 Jahren Bauzeit war der 911 Turbo zum Modelljahreswechsel 1989 endlich ab Werk mit einem Fünfganggetriebe und einer hydraulischen Kupplung erhältlich. Durch die enge Gangabstufung konnte der Ladedruck beim Schalten noch konstanter gehalten werden und die mögliche Beschleunigung aus dem Stand auf Tempo 100 sank um zwei Zehntel auf 5,2 Sekunden. Mit dieser Konfiguration ging der 911 Turbo 3.3 in seine letzte Runde. Als letzter 911 der so genannten »G-Serie« erlebte er die Einführung der Nachfolgergeneration 964 bis auch er zum Modelljahr 1990 endgültig eingestellt wurde.

Porsche 911 Turbo Cabriolet (1987)
Porsche 911 Turbo Cabriolet, 1987

1984, because its engine was not equipped for catalyzer technology. As an alternative, a "Turbo look" 911 Carrera was offered for sale, but this was of course not an ideal alternative to the profitable top model. Work went ahead as a matter of urgency on the Type 965, which was derived from Porsche's 959 model and planned as a replacement for the Turbo 3.3 in the top market segment. With a 360-hp twin-turbo engine and digital engine management, the Type 965 was to be capable of complying with even the toughest environmental protection laws, but in 1988 the project was halted by a model policy decision. Faced with the choice of losing the 911 Turbo's important US market or supplying a model with reduced power output, the engineers chose the latter alternative and produced a "detoxed" export version in 1985 with modified mixture preparation system, closed-loop catalytic converter, lambda oxygen probe and secondary air injection. Despite these measures the US engine, which ran on unleaded gasoline, developed 285 hp.

At the end of 1988, when the next model year was about to appear, many Turbo customers found that one of their long-term dreams had come true:

after having been in production for 14 years the 911 became available with a five-speed gearbox and a hydraulically operated clutch. The close ratios helped to keep turbocharger boost pressure more constant during gear shifts, and acceleration from 0 to 100 (62 mph) improved by a fifth of a second, to 5.2 seconds. This was the configuration in which the 911 Turbo 3.3 entered the ring for its final round. The last of the "G Series" 911s, it continued in production after the next Type 964 generation had been launched, and was not finally discontinued until the 1990 model year.

Phantomzeichnung
911 Turbo 3.3 (1989)
Ghosted drawing
911 Turbo 3.3, 1989

Reifestadium: Porsche 911
Turbo 3.3 (Modelljahr 1989)
*Maturity: Porsche 911 Turbo
3.3 (1989 model year)*

RECHTE SEITE: Rechtslenker:
Innenraum eines 911 Turbo
3.3 (Modelljahr 1989)
RIGHT PAGE: *Interior of
a right-hand-drive 911
Turbo 3.3 (1989 model year)*

SO BAUT MAN SPORTWAGEN –
DIE TURBO-GENERATION 964
HOW SPORTS CARS SHOULD BE BUILT –
THE 964 TURBO MODEL GENERATION

SO BAUT MAN SPORTWAGEN –
DIE TURBO-GENERATION 964
HOW SPORTS CARS SHOULD BE BUILT –
THE 964 TURBO MODEL GENERATION

Zum 25-jährigen Jubiläum des Neunelfers läutete der im November 1988 präsentierte, Allrad angetriebene Porsche 911 Carrera 4 (Typ 964) eine neue Generation des Erfolgsmodells ein. Nach fünfzehn Jahren Bauzeit wurde die so genannte »G-Serie« des 911 zu mehr als 85 Prozent überarbeitet, so dass Porsche ein modernes und marktfähiges Fahrzeug anbieten konnte. Mit der Typenreihe 964 nahm Porsche eine Neupositionierung des 911 vor, mit der das unter wirtschaftlichem Druck stehende Unternehmen der zunehmenden Konkurrenz im Sportwagensegment begegnen wollte.

Der Ideologie der Variantenvielfalt blieb Porsche auch bei der Typenreihe 964 weiterhin treu. In gewohnter Porsche-Manier wurde der neue 911 nach und nach

1990 präsentierte Porsche einen neuen 911 Turbo (964)
Porsche introduced a new 911 Turbo (the Type 964) in 1990

On the occasion of the 911's 25th anniversary in November 1988, the latest generation of this successful model was ushered in by the Porsche 911 Carrera 4 (the Type 964) with all-wheel drive. After a 15-year production period, the 911 "G Series" was thoroughly revised, with changes to more than 85 percent of the car's structure and components. Porsche then had a modern product for modern customers. With the Type 964, Porsche repositioned the 911 on the market and declared its intention, although facing severe economic pressure at the time, to compete successfully against an increasing number of rivals on the sports-car market.

For the Type 964 models, Porsche retained its multi-version model policy. In the customary Porsche

in verschiedenen Karosserie-Versionen und Motorisierungen angeboten. Neben dem Carrera 4 war ab dem Modelljahr 1990 auch der heckgetriebene 911 Carrera 2 erhältlich; neben dem Coupé standen auch eine Cabriolet- und Targa-Version im Verkaufsprogramm. Im darauf folgenden Jahr rundete ein neuer 911 Turbo das Angebot nach oben ab. Auf dem Genfer Salon 1990 stand eine Turbo-Version des 964, die mit breiter Karosserie und dem typischen Heckflügel an die Tradition der 1989 eingestellten Turbo-Elfer anknüpfte. Die zentralen Forderungen während seiner Entwicklung lauteten: Höhere Leistung und Erfüllung strengster Abgasnormen.

Als Antrieb diente der bewährte, jedoch überarbeitete 3,3-Liter-Turbomotor, der einen serienmäßigen Dreiwege-Metall-Katalysator erhielt. Eine Besonderheit war das mit einem Katalysator und Schalldämpfer ausgerüstete Bypass-Endrohr. Die durch den Bypass geleiteten Abgase mussten nicht mehr durch den regulären Katalysator geleitet werden, so dass kein zusätzlicher Staudruck auftrat. Das Ergebnis der Maßnahmen: Die Motorleistung stieg spürbar auf 320 PS, wofür ein auf geringe Strömungsverluste ausgelegtes

Das Turbo-Triebwerk des 964 leistete 320 PS bei 5.750/min
The Type 964's turbocharged engine developed 320 hp at 5750 rpm

RECHTE SEITE: Als erster 911 trug der Turbo ovale Cup-Außenspiegel
RIGHT PAGE: *This Turbo was the first 911 to have oval Cup-style outside mirrors*

fashion, the new 911 appeared step by step with various body styles and power outputs. The 911 Carrera 2 with rear-wheel drive was introduced alongside the Carrera 4 in the 1990 model year, and as well as the Coupe, customers were offered the Convertible and Targa. A year later it was time for a new 911 Turbo to round off the top end of the program. Porsche exhibited a turbocharged version of the Type 964 at the 1990 Geneva Motor Show. With its wide body and typical rear wing, it continued the tradition of turbocharged 911 models that had been interrupted in 1989. The central development requirements were quite clear: higher power and compliance with even the most restrictive exhaust emission laws.

The power unit was familiar, though revised in many respects: the well-proven 3.3-liter turbocharged engine. It was given a closed-loop metal catalytic converter as standard equipment. Another interesting feature was the bypass tailpipe, with its own catalytic converter and muffler. Exhaust gas diverted through the bypass did not pass through the main converter, so that excess back pressure was avoided. As a

Porsche Typ 911 Turbo
(Modelljahr 1991)
*The Porsche 911 Turbo
(1991 model year)*

Ansaugsystem und ein größerer Ladeluftkühler verantwortlich waren. Eine neue Turbinengeometrie bot ein verbessertes Ansprechverhalten bei niedrigen Drehzahlen. An der Motorperipherie wurden zudem die vollelektronische Kennfeld-Zündanlage mit Lambdaregelung und das K-Jetronic-Einspritzsystem in Richtung Kraftstoffeinsparung und Abgasemission modifiziert. Durch den Einbau eines Zweimassen-Schwungrads erreichten die Porsche-Ingenieure dank optimierter Geräusch- und Schwingungsdämpfung zudem einen wesentlich besseren Komfort. Das erstarkte 3,3-Liter-Aggregat beschleunigte den 964 in 5,2 Sekunden auf 100 km/h, die Höchstgeschwindigkeit stieg auf 270 Stundenkilometer. Noch leistungsfähiger als der Motor war die Turbo-Bremsanlage, die den Wagen aus 100 km/h in 2,8 Sekunden in den Stand auf Tempo Null verzögerte.

Unter der klassischen Turbo-Karosserie arbeitete ein neu entwickeltes Fahrwerk mit spurkorrigierender Schräglenker-Hinterachse, deren innere Schräglenkerarme die Fahrstabilität sowohl beim Geradeauslauf als auch bei Richtungs- und Lastwechseln verbesserten. Daneben sorgten eine optimierte McPherson-Feder-

result of these measures, power output went up considerably to 320 hp, with low flow losses in the intake system and a larger charge-air intercooler also playing their part. New turbine geometry improved low-speed engine response. Peripheral changes to the engine included modifications to the all-electronic mapped-characteristic ignition with oxygen sensing by lambda probe and the K-Jetronic fuel injection, with the aims of saving fuel and reducing pollutant emissions. By adopting a double-mass flywheel, Porsche's engineers reduced noise and vibration, making the car as a whole more refined. The uprated 3.3-liter engine proved capable of accelerating the Type 964 from 0 to 100 kph (62 mph) in 5 seconds; the top speed rose to 270 kph (168 mph). Performance of the Turbo's brakes was even more impressive than that of the engine: the car could be brought to a standstill from 100 kph (62 mph) in a mere 2.8 seconds.

Under the classic Turbo body, the suspension was new, with toe-correcting semi-trailing arms at the rear. The layout of the inner arms improved stability in a straight line, when changing direction

bein-Vorderachse mit serienmäßiger Servolenkung und Antiblockier-System für ein harmonisches Fahrgefühl. Erstmals beim Turbo wurde auch ein Sperrdifferential für die Fahrdynamik eingesetzt: Die Sperrwirkung von 20 Prozent im Zug und 100 Prozent im Schub bewirkte beim Lastwechsel, zum Beispiel beim Gaswegnehmen in Kurven, eine für jeden Fahrer kontrollierbare Reaktion. Die 17-Zoll großen Aluminiumräder im Cup-Design leisteten ebenfalls einen entsprechenden Beitrag zur Fahrstabilität.

Neben der Faszination des Fahrens wollte Porsche mit dem neuen Turbo-Modell auch in den Fächern Wirtschaftlichkeit und Vernunft überzeugen. Als einziger Hochleistungssportwagen verband der Porsche die Forderungen nach Alltagstauglichkeit, Funktionalität, Sicherheit und Umweltverträglichkeit. Auch beim 911 Turbo gab Porsche eine Zweijahres-Garantie ohne Kilometerbegrenzung, eine Zehnjahres-Garantie gegen Durchrostung und lange Wartungsintervalle von 20.000 Kilometern. Hinzu kam sein niedriger Wertverlust – der geringste aller Sportwagen. Bei der Insassensicherheit war der 911 Turbo ebenfalls führend und erfüllte mit seinen hochfesten Sicherheits-

suddenly and during load reversals. At the front, optimized McPherson struts combined with standard power steering and the antilock braking system for harmonious handling. This Turbo also had a limited-slip differential to enhance its already dynamic road behavior. The locking action of 20 percent in traction and 100 percent when coasting ensured a controllable reaction, for instance if the driver lifted off at the gas pedal halfway through a bend. 17-inch aluminum wheels of Cup design also contributed to the car's exceptional stability on the move.

As well as the fascination of driving the new Turbo model, Porsche wanted it to be convincing in the economy and common-sense areas. A Porsche is the only high-performance sports car that also satisfies the demands of everyday driving, functional efficiency, safety and environmental acceptability. The 911 Turbo carried Porsche's two-year warranty with no distance limit and a ten-year warranty against rust penetration. The maintenance intervals were generous too, at 20,000 kilometers (app. 12,425 miles). And the Porsche suffered a lower loss of value on the secondhand market than any other sports car. The

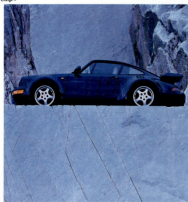

Werbeanzeige »Blue Chip« (1991)
"Blue Chip" advertisement (1991)

911 Turbo led the way in occupant protection: with its high-strength seat belts, its integral bumper system and its plastic safety-design fuel tank, it complied with the safety laws in force all over the world. In the summer of 1991, Porsche again set new standards when all models were given driver's and front passenger's airbags as standard equipment.

As for the previous model, Porsche's Exclusive department was able to offer increased power output for the Turbo. If customers checked order code X33, camshafts with modified valve timing and an inlet manifold and cylinder heads of different pattern were installed. These changes boosted power output from 320 to 355 horsepower. The 911 Turbo Convertible was an even more exclusive offer; only a few were built to customers' special order. Including the power hike, this conversion cost almost 80,000 Deutschmarks (DM).

The 911 Turbo S, exhibited at the Geneva show in the spring of 1992, was the most powerful roadgoing 911 Turbo model seen until then. It was based on the car driven by Hurley Haywood in the Supercar race

gurten, dem integrierten Stoßfängersystem und dem Kunststoff-Sicherheitstank alle weltweit bestehenden Anforderungen. Auch beim Insassenschutz setzte Porsche Maßstäbe, als ab dem Sommer 1991 sämtliche Modelle serienmäßig mit Fahrer- und Beifahrer-Airbags ausgestattet wurden.

Wie bereits beim Vorgängermodell, bot die Abteilung Porsche Exklusiv auch für den 964 Turbo eine Leistungssteigerung an. Kreuzte der Kunde den Bestellcode X33 an, erhielt sein Fahrzeug andere Nockenwellen mit geänderten Steuerzeiten, einen modifizierten Einlaufkrümmer und überarbeitete Zylinderköpfe. Durch diese Maßnahmen stieg die Leistung von 320 auf 355 PS. Noch exklusiver war das 911 Turbo Cabriolet, von dem nur einige wenige Exemplaren gebaut wurden. Allein der Umbaupreis der auf speziellen Kundenwunsch gefertigten Spezialität betrug inklusive Leistungssteigerung fast 80.000 DM.

Die Leistungsspitze aller 911 Turbo-Modelle mit 3,3-Liter Motor markierte jedoch der im Frühjahr 1992 in Genf präsentierte 911 Turbo S. Er basierte auf dem 1991 von Hurley Haywood erfolgreich in der »Super-

Porsche 911 turbo
(Modelljahr 1992)
*Porsche 911 Turbo (1992
model year)*

car«-Rennserie eingesetzten 911 Turbo. Die Straßen-version war äußerlich an den seitlichen Lufteinlässen in den Fondseitenteilen und dem flacheren Heckflügel zu erkennen, in Ausstattung und Gewicht wurde er um 180 Kilogramm radikal reduziert. Eine geänderte Nockenwelle, bearbeitete Ansaugwege, leicht erhöhter Ladedruck und eine optimierte Zünd- und Einspritz-anlage steigerten die Leistung auf 381 PS. Genug für eine Beschleunigung von Null auf 100 km/h in 4,6 Se-kunden und eine Spitze von 290 Stundenkilometern. Einziger Wermutstropfen der in 86 Einheiten gebauten Sonderserie: der Preis in Höhe von 295.000 DM.

Der 911 Turbo der Generation 964 begeisterte von Beginn an. Trotz eines Preises von 182.000 Mark war die Jahresproduktion bereits im Voraus abverkauft. Dass der neue 911 Turbo gut ankommen würde, war bereits auf der Presse-Fahrvorstellung in Südfrank-reich ersichtlich: Sechs der 20 Porsche Turbo, die Porsche zur Präsentation nach St. Paul de Vence gebracht hatte, wurden von Ganoven geklaut.

LINKE SEITE: Als erster Porsche stand der 911 Turbo S auf dreiteiligen 18-Zoll Felgen

Beim Turbo S herrschte Leichtbau auch im Innen-raum
Weight-saving principles were applied to the interior of the Turbo S

Der 3,3 Liter-Turbomotor leistete 381 PS bei einem Drehmoment von 490 Nm
The turbocharged 3.3-liter engine developed 381 hp and a peak torque of 490 Nm

series. The road version could be identified externally by air inlets in the rear side panels and a less steep rear wing. The equipment specification was radically reduced, saving 180 kilograms (397 lbs) in weight. A modified camshaft profile, machined intake ports, a slight increase in turbocharger boost pressure and an optimized ignition and fuel injection system together put the power output up to 381 hp, enough for a 0–100 kph (62 mph) sprint in 4.6 seconds and a top speed of 290 kph (180 mph). The only catch: each of the cars in this special series – and only 86 were built – was billed at 295,000 DM.

The 964-generation 911 Turbo was enthusiastically received from the first moment on. Although the list price was 182,000 DM, a whole year's production was sold in advance. For rather unusual evidence of the new 911 Turbo's popularity, one need only look at the driving event held for journalists in the South of France: Porsche brought 20 Porsche Turbos to Saint Paul de Vence, but thieves made off with six of them!

LEFT PAGE: *The 911 Turbo S was the first Porsche to be shod with three-piece 18-inch wheels*

LEISTUNGSTRÄGER: DER 911 TURBO 3.6

Im letzten Modelljahr der 911-Typenreihe 964 bewies
Porsche einmal mehr, welches Entwicklungspotenzial
im Turbokonzept steckte: Auf dem Pariser Auto-
salon stand im Oktober 1992 der überarbeitete 911
Turbo 3.6. Sein neuer Antrieb mit 3,6 Liter Hubraum
basierte auf dem bereits in der 911 Basisversion
eingesetzten Sechszylinder-Boxermotor, der seine
Standfestigkeit inzwischen im Carrera Cup gezeigt
hatte. Zwangsbeatmet leistete der Motor 360 PS
bei einem maximalen Drehmoment von 520 Newtonmetern, was nicht nur den Fahrleistungen zugute
kam, sondern in der Praxis sogar einen geringeren
Kraftstoffverbrauch ermöglichte. Bei der Entwicklung
des Motors ging es weniger um die Höchstleistung,
denn der Schub im oberen Drehzahlbereich bei vollem
Ladedruck war auch schon vorher so eindrucksvoll,
dass kein Turbo-Fahrer etwas daran auszusetzen
hatte. Auf Landstraßen oder im Stadtverkehr bewegt,
war mehr Drehmoment im unteren Bereich jedoch
sehr willkommen. Durch den vergrößerten Hubraum
profitierte nicht nur das Grund-Drehmoment, auch der
Ladedruck-Aufbau begann nun früher. Das Ergebnis

Porsche 911 Turbo 3.6
(Modelljahr 1993)
*Porsche 911 Turbo 3.6
(1993 model year)*

SOURCE OF ALL POWER: THE 911 TURBO 3.6

As the 911 Type 964 model line reached its final year
of production, Porsche demonstrated once again just
how much development potential the turbocharging
concept possessed. The revised 911 Turbo 3.6 went
on display in October 1992 at the Paris Motor Show.
The new 3.6-liter engine was based on the flat six
used in the standard 911, which had demonstrated
its strength and reliability in Carrera Cup races.
Now came the version with forced aspiration, rated
at 360 horsepower and with a maximum torque of
520 Newton-meters. This engine not only promised
outstanding performance figures, but also proved
to be more economical than its predecessor.
Development work had concentrated less on ultimate
power, since in the upper engine-speed range and
at full boost pressure this was already impressive
enough to satisfy every Turbo driver. But for cross-
country journeys or in city traffic, the increase in
torque at lower speeds was welcome. As well as
developing more torque, the larger engine built up its
boost pressure more rapidly. The turbocharger came
on stream more smoothly and began to produce its

war ein weicheres Einsetzen des Turboladers, der nun schon bei mittleren Drehzahlen den charakteristischen Schub entfaltete.

Der typischen Look der breiten Turbo-Karosserie mit dem großen Heckflügel erhielt einen weiteren Akzent durch ein geändertes Heck-Mittelteil und rote Brems-zangen. Ein prestigeträchtiger Schriftzug »Turbo 3.6« und in die Fondlehnen eingewebte Schriftzüge vervollständigten die neue Turbo-Optik. Bei dem auf die gestiegene Motorleistung abgestimmten Fahr-werk kamen dreiteilige 18-Zoll Speedline-Felgen zum Einsatz, die zusammen mit der geänderten Feder- und Dämpferabstimmung und der optimierten Bremsanla-ge Fahrpräzision und Sicherheit weiter erhöhten. Das Gefühl präziser Dirigierbarkeit und direkter Reaktion auf Lenkbewegungen wurde durch ein um 20 Milli-meter tiefer gelegtes Fahrwerk nochmals erhöht.

In Verbindung mit der Unterbodenverkleidung bis zum Motor und den strömungsgünstigen Cup-Außenspiegeln konnte der Turbo 3.6 auch mit einer ausgewogenen Aerodynamik punkten. Mit dem Auftriebs-Idealwert Null, auf cW 0,35 reduziertem Luft-

LINKE SEITE: Der 911 Turbo 3.6 rollte auf dreiteiligen 18-Zoll Felgen
LEFT PAGE: *The 911 Turbo 3.6 was fitted with three-piece 18-inch wheels*

Der 3,6-Liter-Turbomotor leistete 360 PS
The 3.6-liter turbocharged engine had a power output of 360 hp

typical extra thrust at moderate engine speeds. Further visual accents were added to the typical extra-wide Turbo body with its large rear wing: the central section of the tail end was modified, and red brake calipers were installed. The prestigious badge now read "Turbo 3.6" and lettering woven into the rear seat backs completed the new Turbo look. The suspension settings were modified to cope with the increased power, and the three-piece 18-inch Speedline wheels, together with the modified spring and shock absorber settings and the optimized brake system made a further contribution to directional precision and safety. This feeling of precise direc-tional control and direct response to steering wheel movements was further enhanced by lowering the body by 20 millimeters (0.8 inch).

With an undertray extending back as far as the engine, and low-drag Cup-style outside mirrors, the Turbo 3.6's well-balanced aerodynamics were much praised. The drag coefficient (c_D) was reduced to 0.35 (at the time a value not matched by other sports cars, the ideal figure being of course zero), and the frontal area lowered. With its high power output, the

Porsche 911 Turbo 3.6
(Modelljahr 1993)
*Porsche 911 Turbo 3.6
(1993 model year)*

widerstandsbeiwert und geringer Querschnittsfläche war er zu seiner Zeit führend in der Sportwagenwelt. Als Folge des hohen Leistungspotenzials erreichte der 911 Turbo eine Spitzengeschwindigkeit von 280 km/h, Tempo 100 wurde aus stehendem Start nach 4,8 Sekunden erreicht. Dennoch wurde gegenüber dem 3,3-Liter-Vorgängermodell im Teillastbereich eine Kraftstoffeinsparung von bis zu 10 Prozent ermöglicht.

Bei aller Leistungs-Überlegenheit behielt auch der 911 Turbo 3.6 seine typische Universalität: Ein Ausnahme-Sportwagen der Spitzenklasse, der für wettbewerbsmäßiges Fahren ebenso geeignet war, wie für den starken Auftritt auf dem Boulevard.

Aber auch auf der Rennstrecke machte der 911 Turbo der Typenreihe 964 eine gute Figur. Nachdem der 911 Turbo bereits 1991 und 1992 den Titel in der amerikanischen Rennserie »IMSA Supercar« gewonnen hatte, ging 1993 auch die 3,6-Liter-Version an den Start, um sich gegen Seriensportwagen vom Schlage eines Honda NSX oder Corvette ZR1 zu beweisen. Mit Ausnahme einer geänderten Auspuffanlage, strafferen Federn und Dämpfern und einem Sicherheitskäfig ging

Meisterlich: Hans-Joachim Stuck im Porsche 911 Turbo 3.6 IMSA Supercar (1993)
Masterly: Hans-Joachim Stuck in the Porsche 911 Turbo 3.6 IMSA Supercar (1993)

PORSCHE

Triumph ★ in USA ´93

1. Porsche	173	Punkte
2. Lotus	145	Punkte
3. Pontiac	111	Punkte
4. BMW	105	Punkte
5. Chevrolet	102	Punkte

1. Hans-Joachim Stuck, Porsche	212	Punkte
2. Doc Bundy, Lotus	162	Punkte
Andy Pilgrim, Lotus	162	Punkte
4. Hurley Haywood, Porsche	161	Punkte
5. Mike Gagliardo, Pontiac	141	Punkte

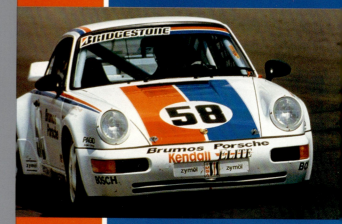

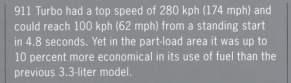

Porsche 911 Turbo 3.6
IMSA Supercar (1993)
*Porsche 911 Turbo 3.6 IMSA
Supercar (1993)*

911 Turbo had a top speed of 280 kph (174 mph) and could reach 100 kph (62 mph) from a standing start in 4.8 seconds. Yet in the part-load area it was up to 10 percent more economical in its use of fuel than the previous 3.3-liter model.

Although endowed with such massive power, the 911 Turbo 3.6 remained a thoroughly "usable" car: an exceptional top-class sports car just as suitable for use in competition as for relaxed driving on the world's fashionable boulevards.

On the racetrack, the Type 964 version of the 911 Turbo put up an impressive performance. Following 1991 and 1992, in which the 911 Turbo took the American IMSA Supercar series title, the 3.6-liter version was sent to the starting line in the 1993 season, where it had to contend with production sports cars such as the Honda NSX and Corvette ZR1. Apart from a modified exhaust system, firmer springs and shocks and the obligatory safety roll cage, the 911 Turbo 3.6 IMSA Supercar entry was entirely standard in its specification. After no fewer than seven successive wins, the result was beyond

der 911 Turbo 3.6 IMSA-Supercar vollkommen serienmäßig an den Start. Nach einer Serie von sieben Siegen in Folge standen Porsche und Hans-Joachim Stuck
als Gewinner der Marken- und Fahrermeisterschaft der
Supercar-Serie fest.

Für Langstreckenrennen nach GT-Reglement bot
Porsche 1993 mit dem 911 Turbo S Le Mans GT eine
echte Rennversion an. Das Fahrzeug entstand in der
Weissacher Rennabteilung und wurde an Kundenteams
verkauft, die bei Langstreckenrennen in der neu ge-
schaffenen GT-Klasse starten wollten. Als Pionier der
Turbo-Technik entschied sich Porsche für den Einsatz
eines Biturbo-Motors mit 3,16 Liter Hubraum, der
trotz Air-Restriktor 474 PS leistete. Eine Besonderheit
gegenüber früheren 911-Rennwagen war die Frischluft-
ansaugung über die Außenseiten des Heckflügels. Die
Premiere und Erprobung des neuen GT-Rennwagens
fand beim 12 Stunden-Rennen von Sebring statt. Das
Fahrer-Trio Walter Röhrl, Hans-Joachim Stuck und Hurley Haywood holten mit dem 911 Turbo S Le Mans GT
nicht nur den Klassensieg, sondern fuhren mit einem
siebten Gesamtrang mitten in das Feld der C-Wagen
hinein.

Testfahrt des 911 Turbo S
Le Mans GT
in Paul Ricard (1992)
*Test-driving the 911 Turbo S
Le Mans GT at the
Paul Ricard circuit (1992)*

doubt: Porsche and Hans-Joachim Stuck had won the
Supercar series manufacturer's and driver's titles.

For long-distance races run according to GT rules,
Porsche produced a genuine racing version in
1993: the 911 Turbo S Le Mans GT. It was built by
the competition department in Weissach, and sold
to customer teams who wanted to enter for long-
distance races in the GT class that had just been
created. As a pioneer in turbocharging technology,
Porsche decided on a 3.16-liter engine with twin
turbochargers; despite the intake air restrictor
called for by the rules, this engine developed
474 horsepower. An interesting technical feature that
differed from previous 911 racecars: intake air was
drawn in at the outer extremities of the rear wing.
The new GT racing car war premiered and had its
first trial outing at the 12-hour race in Sebring. The
three 911 Turbo S Le Mans GT drivers Walter Röhrl,
Hans-Joachim Stuck and Hurley Haywood not only won
their class but came seventh overall, well up the field
of C-class cars.

Interieur des 911 Turbo S
Le Mans GT
*Interior of the 911 Turbo S
Le Mans GT*

RECHTE SEITE:
Der 476 PS-Motor verfügte
über Digitale-Motor-Elek-
tronik und sequentielle
Einspritzung
RIGHT PAGE: *The 476-hp
engine had Digital Motor
Electronics and sequential
fuel injection*

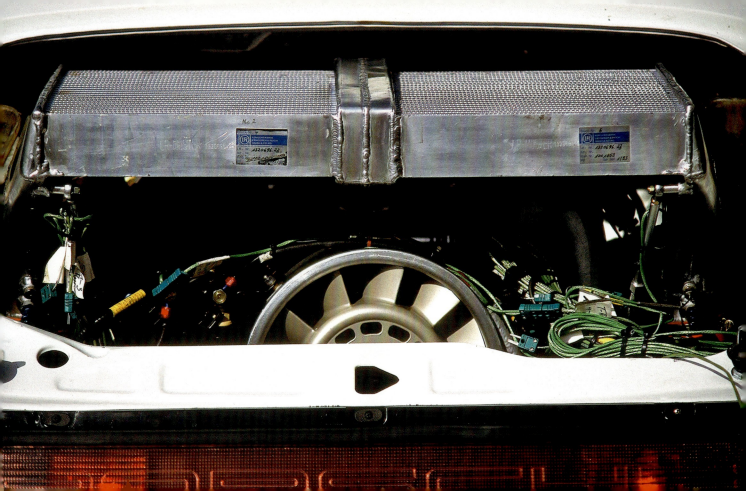

911% FAHRSPASS – DIE TURBO-GENERATION 993
911% DRIVING FUN – THE 993 TURBO GENERATION

911% FAHRSPASS – DIE TURBO-GENERATION 993
911% DRIVING FUN – THE 993 TURBO GENERATION

30 Jahre nach seiner ersten Präsentation und nach mehr als 350.000 verkauften Exemplaren bewies der Porsche 911 zum Modelljahr 1994 einmal mehr seine Modernität und Entwicklungsfähigkeit. Auf der Frankfurter IAA fand im September 1993 die Weltpremiere des Porsche 911 Carrera der Typenreihe 993 statt. Mit seinen breiten und geradlinig verlaufenden Kotflügeln sowie den neuen Ellipsoid-Scheinwerfern wurde erstmals in der Geschichte des 911 das Design deutlich verändert. Und auch technisch war der neue Elfer ein großer Sprung nach vorne: Bereits das Basismodell 911 Carrera leistete 272 PS und lief 270 km/h. Sein neues Fahrwerk nach dem »LSA-Prinzip« (Leichtbau, Stabilität, Agilität) nahm dem heckmotorisierten Elfer endgültig seine Tücke. Mit Spannung wurde erwartet, was eine Turbo-Version bringen würde.

Der neue 911 Carrera feierte 1993 Weltpremiere
The new 911 Carrera was presented in 1993

30 years after its initial presentation and with more than 350,000 sold, the 1994 model year was a further opportunity for the Porsche 911 to display its modernity and scope for ongoing development. The German "IAA" Motor Show in Frankfurt, held in September 1993, was the venue for the world premiere of the Type 993 Porsche 911 Carrera. The wide fenders extending back in a straight line and the new ellipsoidal headlamps were the first major design changes in the history of the 911. Technically too, the 911 was about to take a major step forward: even the basic Carrera version had a power output of 272 hp and could reach a top speed of 270 kph (168 mph). Its new suspension, with the LSA principle (light weight, stability, agility) as its motto finally put a stop to any handling and control problems that might still have

Nach einer einjährigen Produktionspause des Turbo-Modells wurde im März 1995 einen neue Version des Supersportwagens mit Allradantrieb vorgestellt. Wie deutlich dieser die Leistungswerte seines Vorgänger-modells übertreffen sollte, geriet zu einer wirklichen Überraschung und bestätigte einmal mehr die Innovationskraft der Porsche-Denkfabrik in Weissach. Für die neue Turbo-Generation standen ehrgeizige Ziele im Lastenheft der Entwicklungsingenieure: exzellentes Fahrverhalten, höchste Fahrstabilität, optimales Handling, beste Traktion und natürlich Leichtbau, denn die verbesserten Fahrleistungen sollten bei reduziertem Verbrauch erreicht werden. Die Realisierung dieser Aufgabe gelang nur mit hohem Entwicklungsaufwand und innovativen Lösungen – auch im Detail.

Das neue Spitzenmodell der 911 Baureihe glänzte mit einem außergewöhnlichen Leistungsangebot von 408 PS, das ein Sechszylinder-Biturbo offerierte. Diese Antriebsleistung erforderte besonders wirkungsvolle Maßnahmen, um ein Höchstmaß an Fahrstabilität auch bei einem Spitzentempo von 290 km/h sicherzustellen. Dazu trug der serienmäßige Allradantrieb ebenso bei, wie eine aufwändige Radführung

Harmonisches Design-konzept: Porsche 911 Turbo (Modelljahr 1996)
Harmonious body styling: Porsche 911 Turbo (model year 1996)

US-Werbeanzeige für den Porsche 911 Turbo (1995)
US advertisement for the Porsche 911 Turbo (1995)

remained on this rear-engined car. Not surprisingly, there was keen interest in how the Turbo version would perform.

In March 1995, after the previous Turbo had been out of production for a year, a new version of this supersport model with all-wheel drive was announced. The degree to which it outperformed its predecessor was a genuine surprise, and confirmed yet again the powers of innovation available from Porsche's "think tank" in Weissach. The new-generation Turbo had to fulfill the ambitious goals the development engineers had written into its requirement specification: excellent road behavior, supreme dynamic stability, optimal handling, reliable traction – and of course weight-saving construction, to ensure that the performance improvements were accompanied by lower fuel consumption. Immense development effort and many brilliantly conceived innovations, including numerous detail design improvements, went into the realization of this task.

The new top model in the 911 line could call upon the exceptional power output of 408 hp from its

Up to 181 mph, to be exact (if you've got your own racetrack). Zero to sixty in just over four heartbeats. 400 horses. Liquid all-wheel drive. It's the new Nine Eleven Turbo. Seriously bad news for the insect world. Call 1-800-PORSCHE and find out why: Porsche. There is no substitute.™

turbo

Kills bugs fast.

und schließlich eine ausgefeilte Aerodynamik. Trotz breiterer Karosserie konnte nicht nur der Luftwiderstandsbeiwert gegenüber dem Vorgänger um einen Punkt gesenkt werden, sondern gleichzeitig auch Auftriebsbeiwerte nahe Null an der Vorder- und Hinterachse realisiert werden. Gute Voraussetzungen für souveränes Fahrverhalten und sichere Übertragung der Antriebs-, Brems- und Seitenkräfte auch bei hohen Geschwindigkeiten.

Der Allradantrieb wurde nicht primär als Anfahrhilfe auf rutschigem Untergrund konzipiert, sondern als wichtiger Beitrag zu noch mehr Fahrsicherheit bei hohen Geschwindigkeiten, bei Regen oder in schwierigen, überraschenden Situationen. Das Allradsystem mit Viscolamellenkupplung verlieh dem 911 Turbo beste Fahrdynamikwerte bei maximaler Traktion. Mindestens fünf Prozent des Motordrehmoments wirkten ständig auf die Vorderachse, was im Extremfall blitzschnell auf bis zu 40 Prozent erhöht wurde. Ein weiteres Plus an aktiver Fahrsicherheit steuerte das fahrdynamische Sperrensystem mit Sperrdifferential und aktivem Bremsdifferential (ABD) bei. Außerdem wurde der 911 Turbo serienmäßig mit einem straf-

Phantomzeichnung des 911 Turbo (Modelljahr 1996)
Ghosted drawing of the 911 Turbo (1996 model year)

feren und tiefergelegten Fahrwerk ausgestattet. Stilistisch orientierte sich der neue 911 Turbo an den Carrera-Modellen der Typenreihe 993, markierte aber durch sein eigenständiges Design seine motorische, wie fahrdynamische Potenz. Die hinteren Kotflügel wurden gegenüber dem Vorgänger noch einmal verbreitert und die seitlichen Schwellerblenden in das Fondseitenteil integriert. Im Bugteil vergrößerten die Techniker die Lufteinlässe, um den erhöhten Kühlbedarf des starken Motors abzudecken. Getreu der Devise »Form follows function« gestalteten die Porsche-Stilisten unter Leitung von Harm Lagaay auch einen neuen Heckflügel, der sich harmonisch in das dynamische Fahrzeugdesign einfügte und für den entscheidenden Stabilisierungseffekt im Heckbereich sorgte. Die Funktionsanforderungen an den neuen Flügel führten bei der Produktion zum erstmaligen Einsatz des RTM-Verfahrens (Resin-Transfer-Moulding). Dabei wurde der gesamte Hohlkörper des Heckdeckel-spoilers in einem Stück hergestellt. Das Entwicklungs-ziel Leichtbau wurde beim Turbo-Heckspoiler ebenso erreicht wie die übrigen Funktionsanforderungen. Gegenüber dem Vorgängermodell betrug die Gewichts-reduzierung immerhin 50 Prozent.

Der neue 911 Turbo wirkte noch kraftvoller und muskulöser
The rear view of the new 911 Turbo was even more powerful and muscular

Der Heckspoiler des 993 Turbo war ganz in Wagenfarbe lackiert
The rear spoiler for the Type 993 Turbo was painted entirely in the body color

six-cylinder twin-turbo engine. With so much power available, effective measures were needed to maintain a high degree of dynamic stability at speeds that could reach 290 kph (180 mph). All-wheel drive as standard equipment had a major contribution to make, as well as complex suspension design and carefully crafted aerodynamics. Although the body was wider, it proved possible to lower the drag coefficient by one decimal point and at the same time to keep front- and rear-axle lift values down almost to zero – excellent preconditions for supremely confident driving and reliable absorption of tractive, braking and lateral dynamic forces even at high speeds.

The car's all-wheel drive system was not intended primarily as a traction aid on low-grip surfaces, but as an important contribution to safety at high speeds, in wet weather or in difficult, unexpected situations. The all-wheel-drive system, with its multi-plate viscous coupling, gave the 911 Turbo excellent road dynamics as well as maximum traction. At least five percent of engine torque was supplied permanently to the front axle, but the figure could be increased instantly to as much as 40 percent in extreme situations. For still

Stark, Schön, Schnell:
Porsche 911 Turbo
(Modelljahr 1997)
*Strong, beautiful and fast:
the Porsche 911 Turbo
(1997 model year)*

Der neue 911 Turbo verkörpert eine Idee pur.

Es ist die Idee Leistung.

Und zwar in allen Bereichen.

Er ist unser Angebot an Fahrer, die eine Leistung fordern,

die sie selbst bereit sind zu geben.

PORSCHE

Werbeanzeige für den
Porsche 911 Turbo (1995)
*Advertisement for the
Porsche 911 Turbo (1995)*

Neben dem Heckspoiler war der 993 Turbo optisch durch seine Räder im Design eines Turbinen-Schaufelrads gekennzeichnet. Als Weltneuheit wurden die 18-Zoll großen Aluminium-Felgen in Hohlspeichen-Technik ausgeführt, wodurch pro Felge drei Kilogramm Gewicht gespart wurden. Bei der Fertigung der Hightech-Räder setzte Porsche auf das Verfahren der Reibschweißung: Felge und Schüssel waren getrennte Bauelemente, die erst durch einen speziellen Schweißvorgang unlösbar miteinander verbunden wurden. Trotz geringerem Gewichts ließ sich dadurch eine höhere Bauteilsteifigkeit erzielen. Diese erhebliche Reduzierung der ungefederten Massen kam nicht zuletzt auch dem Fahrverhalten zugute. In Kombination mit den leichten Hohlspeichenfelgen trug auch die standfeste, renntaugliche Bremsanlage zur außerordentlichen Dynamik des 911 Turbo bei. Dank der großen Bremse mit ABS 5 verzögerte der Turbo aus Tempo 200 in nur 4,5 Sekunden – dies entsprach einer maximalen Bremsleistung von 1.941 PS.

Die eigentliche Revolution des neuen Turbo war jedoch die Kombination aus 408 PS und dem fahrdynamischen Allradantrieb. Ganz im Stile eines klassischen

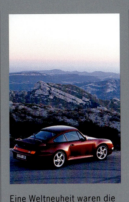

Eine Weltneuheit waren die Hohlspeichen-Aluminiumfelgen
Hollow-spoke wheels were used for the first time on a production vehicle

greater active safety, there was a dynamic differential lock system and an active brake differential (ABD), and in addition, the 911 Turbo was equipped as standard with firmer suspension settings and a lowered body.

In its styling the new 911 Turbo took its cue from the Type 993 Carrera models, but was sufficiently different to emphasize its power and dynamism. Compared with the previous model the body width at the rear was increased again, and the side sill trims integrated into the rear fenders. At the front, the engineers called for larger air intakes to satisfy the engine's increased cooling requirements. True to the motto "form follows function", the stylists led by Harm Lagaay created a new rear wing that blended harmoniously into the car's dynamic overall design and generated the essential stabilizing effect at the rear. The functional requirements that the new wing had to satisfy led to the use of the RTM (Resin Transfer Molding) process for the first time. The entire hollow element of this spoiler, for attachment to the rear engine cover, was manufactured as a single piece, and met the requirement for light weight as

Gran Turismo ließen sich im 911 Turbo entspannt und souverän hohe Reiseschnitte erzielen. Wenn er aber gefordert wurde, stieß er mit seinen Fahrleistungen in Extrembereiche vor, die Mitte der neunziger Jahre mit kaum einem anderen Auto möglich waren. Schon gar nicht mit der Porsche-typischen Alltagstauglichkeit. Der mit zwei kleinen Turboladern bestückte 3,6 Liter-Motor besaß eine Leistungscharakteristik mit einem breiten Drehzahlband, die einem hubraumstarken Saugmotor nicht unähnlich war. Bereits ab 2.000 Umdrehungen entwickelte das Triebwerk reichlich Schub, der sich ab 3.500 /min in ein stürmisches Rasen verwandelte, das die Insassen eindrucksvoll in die Sitze presste. Neben der Leistungssteigerung auf 408 PS und der Anhebung des maximalen Drehmoments auf 540 Nm hatten die Weissacher Ingenieure auch das Ziel, das »Turbo-Loch« des Motors beim Beschleunigen auf ein bisher nicht gekanntes Minimum zu reduzieren. Sie erreichten es durch den Einsatz zweier kleiner, statt eines großen Abgasturboladers, wobei sich vor allem das Trägheitsmoment der kleineren Rotoren auswirkte. Die beiden geregelten Turbinen mit integrierter Bypasslappe erzeugten einen Ladedruck von 0,8 bar. Die eindrucksvolle Leistungs- und Drehmomentsteige-

Der 3,6-Liter Boxer wurde mit zwei KKK-Turboladern und zwei Ladeluftkühlern ausgestattet
The 3.6-liter flat-six engine had two KKK turbochargers and two charge-air intercoolers

well as the functional exigencies. Compared with the previous version, the weight saving was no less than 50 percent.

In addition to the rear spoiler, the 993 Turbo was visually notable for its hi-tech 18-inch aluminum wheels with turbine-blade styling. They were manufactured with hollow spokes, a first on the world market that made each wheel three kilograms (6.6 lbs) lighter. Porsche joined the rim to the wheel center permanently by a special friction welding technique that avoided excess unsprung weight but made the wheel extremely rigid, both factors that improved the car's road behavior still further. Like the lightweight hollow-spoke wheels, the fade-free brake system with its motor-sport background added to the 911 Turbo's exceptional dynamism. The large-diameter brakes with fifth-generation ABS were capable of halting the car in only 4.5 seconds from 200 kph (124 mph), equivalent to an energy dissipation of 1,941 horsepower.

The true revolution set in progress by the Turbo was the combination of 408 horsepower with dynamically controlled all-wheel drive. In the style

Weitere Informationen und die neue Diskette „911 Turbo" erhalten Sie rund um die Uhr von Porsche Online: Telefon und Fax 0137 - 356 911.

Einige sagen, er paßt nicht in diese Zeit.

Andere werfen ihm sein Leistungsvermögen vor.

auto motor und sport nennt ihn den saubersten

Sportwagen Deutschlands.*

Wir meinen, maximale Leistung bei minimalen

Abgaswerten ist eine typische Porsche Lösung.

PORSCHE

Saubermann: Der 911 Turbo war das emissionsärmste Auto seiner Zeit
Clean power: the 911 Turbo had a lower level of exhaust emissions than any other car

of a classic Gran Turismo model, the 911 Turbo covered enormous distances in a supremely relaxed manner and at high average speeds. But if the need arose, it could perform in extreme conditions in a way that scarcely any other car could match in the mid-nineteen-nineties, and certainly not a car with the Porsche's typical day-to-day driving qualities. With its two small turbochargers, the 3.6-liter engine developed its power over a broad speed range not very dissimilar from a large naturally aspirated engine. At 2000 revolutions per minute the engine already developed plenty of thrust, and from 3500 rpm upwards this was transformed into a tumult of power that pressed the car's occupants firmly back into their seats. As well as boosting power output to 408 hp and raising maximum torque to 540 Nm, the engineers in Weissach had pursued an additional goal: to reduce "turbo lag" when accelerating to a previously unattained minimum. Instead of a single large turbocharger they used two smaller units, with rotors incurring only a lower moment of inertia. The two controlled-action turbines with integral bypass flap valve generated a boost pressure of 0.8 bar. Other factors contributing to the impressive increases

rung verdankte der Motor zudem der Optimierung des Ladungswechsels, dem hohen Wirkungsgrad der beiden Ladeluftkühler und der Klopfregelung, die einen Betrieb bei optimalem Wirkungsgrad erlaubte.

Ein weiteres technisches Highlight des Sechszylinders war das neue Abgasüberwachungssystem OBD II. Dieses erlaubte ein frühzeitiges Erkennen von Fehlern oder Defekten im Abgas- und Kraftstoffsystem. Die aufwändigen Maßnahmen zur Schadstoffreduzierung zeigten beim 911 Turbo große Wirkung: Zur Überraschung der Fachwelt entpuppte sich der Turbomotor als emissionsärmster Serien-Automobilantrieb der Welt. Zudem ging der aufgeladene 993 als erster Biturbo mit Luftmassenregelung in die Automobilgeschichte ein. Gemeinsam mit dem leichtesten und effizientesten Allradantrieb dieser Klasse trug auch das überarbeitete Sechsgang-Getriebe dazu bei, einen der Leistung angemessenen Kraftstoffverbrauch und niedrige Abgaswerte zu erreichen. Flott bewegt, bedeutete dies 14 bis 15 Liter, wobei bei einer entspannten Autobahnfahrt auch Verbrauchswerte um 10 Liter pro 100 Kilometer möglich waren. Vorbei waren auch die Zeiten, als ein 911 Turbo als ein hartes Männer-Auto

Turbo-Interieur
(Modelljahr 1996)
*Interior of the Turbo
(1996 model year)*

Der 408 PS Biturbo war
der emissionsärmste Serie-
motor der Welt
*The 408-hp twin-turbo-
charger engine was the
world's lowest-emission car
power unit*

in power output and torque were optimized cylinder filling and discharge, the high efficiency of the two charge air intercoolers and the knock control, which enabled the engine to run closer to the point at which optimum efficiency was achieved.

The six-cylinder engine featured another technical highlight: the OBD II exhaust emission monitoring system, designed to identify malfunctions or defects in the exhaust and fuel systems at an early stage. Although complex, the pollution avoidance measures for the 911 Turbo were extremely effective: to the amazement of experts, the turbocharged unit proved to have the lowest emissions of any series-production automobile engine on the world market. The Type 993 was also the first twin-turbo model with air mass control in the history of the automobile. The lightest and most efficient all-wheel drive train in this performance category and a six-speed gearbox of revised design helped to keep fuel consumption and exhaust emissions down to an acceptable level for such a powerful car. When driven hard, 14 to 15 liters of fuel were consumed per 100 kilometers (15.7–16.8 US, 18.8–20.2 UK mpg), but relaxed

galt. Eine Doppelkonussynchronisierung des ersten und zweiten Gangs reduzierte die Schaltkräfte um bis zu 40 Prozent, eine hydraulische Kupplungsunterstützung die Pedalkraft um 25 Prozent.

Wie bei Porsche üblich, arbeiteten die Ingenieure an weiteren Interpretationen des 911 Turbo Themas. 1995 entstanden bei Porsche Exclusive 14 Exemplare eines Turbo Cabriolets der Generation 993, deren Antriebsstrang und Bremsanlage allerdings noch vom 964 Turbo 3.6 stammten. Ein Jahr darauf bot die Exclusive-Abteilung ein 430 PS-Leistungskit an, das ein modifiziertes Steuergerät und einen zusätzlichen Ölkühler beinhaltete. Für das Modelljahr 1998 gab es für den 911 Turbo ein Sportfahrwerk sowie eine optionale Leistungssteigerung auf 450 PS, mit der nun auch die 300-Stundenkilometer Marke durchbrochen werden konnte. Ein solcher werksseitig leistungsgesteigerter 911 Turbo zog auch mit einem 911 GT2 gleich, der als Kundensportgerät seine Rennambitionen offen zur Schau trug. Noch exklusiver war nur noch der ab August 1997 angebotene 911 Turbo S. Der über 300.000 DM teure Hochleistungssportwagen trug ein Aerokit mit geändertem Front- und Heckspoiler und

Der 911 Turbo S wurde von Porsche Exclusive November 1997 bis April 1998 gebaut
The 911 Turbo S was built by Porsche Exclusive between November 1997 and April 1998

driving on the freeway could easily improve the figure to the region of 10 l/100 km (23.5 US, 28.2 UK mpg). Furthermore, the days when the 911 Turbo was regarded exclusively as a car for "tough guys" were gone forever. Double-cone synchromesh on first and second gears reduced shift effort by as much as 40 percent, and a hydraulically operated clutch cut the pressure needed at the pedal by 25 percent.

Once again, it was typical of Porsche's engineers that they should look into further interpretations of the 911 Turbo topic. In 1995 Porsche Exclusive built 14 993-generation Turbo Convertibles, though with the drive train and brake system from the Type 964 3.6-liter Turbo. A year later the Porsche Exclusive department offered customers a 430-horsepower performance kit, including a modified control unit and an additional oil cooler. For the 1998 model year, sport suspension became available for the 911 Turbo, and also an optional engine upgrade to 450 hp, which enabled the car to break the 300-kph (186-mph) barrier. With this factory-supplied power boost, the 911 Turbo drew level with the 911 GT2, which sold to private motor-sport enthusiasts for racing purposes and in

Lufteinlässen im Fondseitenteil. Im Innenraum verdeut-
lichte ein Voll-Leder-Carbon-Interieur die Exklusivität
des 345-mal gebauten Turbo S.

Angesichts des enormen Leistungspotenzials dauerte
es nicht lange, bis motorsportbegeisterte Fahrer ihren
911 Turbo auch im Rennsport einsetzten. Im Frühjahr
1996 siegten zwei serienmäßige 911 Turbo bei der
australischen »Targa Tasmania«, die in Fachkreisen zu
den härtesten Rallyes der Welt gezählt wurde. Beein-
druckend war auch die Leistung des amerikanischen
Rennfahrers Jeff Zwart. Mit einem Porsche 911 Turbo
S siegte er 1998 beim legendären Bergrennen »Pikes
Peak International Hill Climb« in Colorado, USA.

911 Turbo S vor dem
Schüttgut in Zell am See
*911 Turbo S in front of the
Schüttgut, Zell am See*

visual terms made no secret of its ambitions. The 911
Turbo S, which went on sale in August 1997, was even
more of an exclusive sales proposition. Costing more
than 300,000 DM, this high-performance sports car
had an "Aerokit" with modified front and rear spoilers
and air intakes on the sides of the body toward
the rear. An all-leather and carbon fiber interior
emphasized the exclusive character of the Turbo S, of
which 345 were built.

In view of its enormous performance potential, it was
not long before 911 Turbo owners began to race their
cars. In the spring of 1996 two standard-specification
911 Turbo cars won the "Targa Tasmania" regarded by
experts as one of the world's toughest rallies. Another
impressive performance was put up by American race
driver Jeff Zwart, who won the legendary Pikes Peak
International Hill Climb in Colorado, USA in 1998, at
the wheel of a Porsche 911 Turbo S.

US-Werbeanzeige für den
Porsche 911 Turbo (1995)
US advertisement for the
Porsche 911 Turbo (1995)

LINKE SEITE: Der 911
Turbo S gewann 1998 das
»Pikes Peak«-Bergrennen
LEFT PAGE: *In 1988 the*
911 Turbo S won the
Pikes Peak hill climb

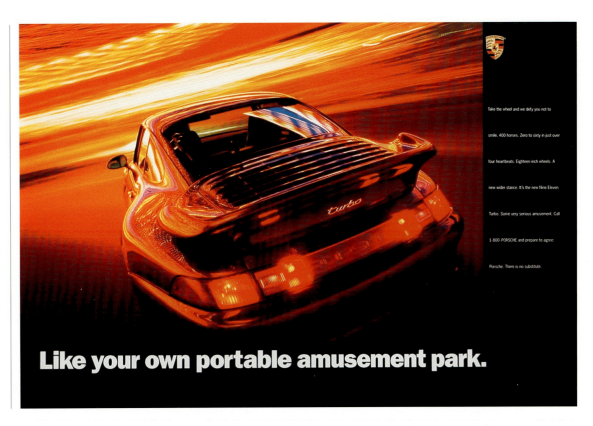

Take the wheel and we defy you not to smile. 400 horses. Zero to sixty in just over four heartbeats. Eighteen inch wheels. A new wider stance. It's the new Nine Eleven Turbo. Some very serious amusement. Call 1-800-PORSCHE and prepare to agree: Porsche. There is no substitute.

Like your own portable amusement park.

EVOLUTION EINES KLASSIKERS – DER 911 TURBO (996)
EVOLUTION OF A CLASSIC – THE 911 TURBO (996)

EVOLUTION EINES KLASSIKERS – DER 911 TURBO (996)
EVOLUTION OF A CLASSIC – THE 911 TURBO (996)

Unter dem Motto »Evolution 911« wurde im September 1997 eine neuer 911 Carrera auf der Frankfurter IAA vorgestellt. Mit dem Übergang vom letzten luftgekühlten 911 zu einer neuen Generation des Sportwagen-Klassikers zeigte Porsche 1997 nicht nur seine Innovationsfähigkeit, sondern setzte auch eine erfolgreiche Entwicklung fort, die ein Jahr zuvor mit dem Boxster begonnen hatte. Als völlige Neuentwicklung wurde die 911-Typenreihe 996 erstmals von einem wassergekühlten Vierventil-Sechszylinder-Boxermotor angetrieben. Obwohl der 996 von der ersten bis zur letzten Schraube neu entwickelt wurde, besaß er alle typischen Merkmale eines Elfers und war gegenüber der Vorgängerbaureihe 993 in nahezu allen Punkten verbessert worden. Bei gleich gebliebenem Preisniveau bot er mehr Leistung, Komfort, Platz, Sicherheit und Ausstattung. Bis zur Präsentation einer Turbo-

Wassergekühlt: 911 Carrera 3,4 (Modelljahr 1998)
With a water-cooled engine: the 911 Carrera 3.4 (1998 model year)

LINKE SEITE: Höhepunkt der Zuffenhausener Produktoffensive: Der 911 Turbo (996)
LEFT PAGE: *Climax of the Zuffenhausen product offensive: the 911 Turbo (Type 996)*

In September 1997, when a new 911 Carrera was exhibited at the German Motor Show in Frankfurt (the "IAA") the motto was "Evolution 911". The last air-cooled 911 made way for the latest generation of this classic sports car, Porsche not only demonstrated its powers of innovation, but also continued along the successful path first taken a year earlier with the Boxster. A totally new development, the Type 996 was powered for the first time by a water-cooled flat-six engine with four valves per cylinder. But although the Type 996 was new almost down to the last nut and screw, it possessed all the typical characteristics of a 911, and improved on the previous Type 993 in just about every way. The price remained unchanged, but the new car offered more of everything: performance, comfort and convenience, interior space, safety and equipment. Only in one respect

Version der 996-Baureihe sollte es allerdings noch zwei Jahre dauern, denn neben modellpolitischen Überlegungen benötigte die Entwicklung des neuen Technologieträgers Zeit. Aus diesem Grund lief die Produktion des luftgekühlten Turbo-Elfers weiter, bis am 24. April 1998 endgültig der letzte Turbo der Typenreihe 993 vom Band lief.

Auf der IAA 1999 war es dann soweit: Passend zum anstehenden 25-jährigen Jubiläum des 911 Turbo präsentierte Porsche eine aufgeladene Version des 996, die Fans und Journalisten einmal mehr mit Hochtechnologie beeindruckte. Im Datenblatt standen 420 PS bei einem Drehmoment von 560 Newtonmetern. Die hohe Leistung und das kraftvolle Drehmoment ermöglichten eine Beschleunigung von Null auf Hundert in 4,2 Sekunden. Mit diesen Werten war der neue Turbo noch schneller als ein GT3 und belegte unter allen 911-Modellen den absoluten Spitzenplatz. Trotz der enormen Motorleistung waren Traktionsprobleme für den 911 Turbo ein Fremdwort, wofür maßgeblich der serienmäßige Allradantrieb verantwortlich war. Der Antrieb der Vorderräder, den weiterhin eine Visco-Kupplung regelte, blieb auf 40

Der neue 911 Turbo wurde 1999 auf der IAA präsentiert
The new 911 Turbo introduced at the 1999 German Motor Show

were the enthusiasts disappointed: two years went by before a Turbo version was introduced. Apart from questions of model policy, time was needed for the development of the technological leader in the 911 model line. For this reason, production of the air-cooled 911 Turbo continued, and it was not until April 24, 1998 that the last Type 993 Turbo left the assembly line.

The great day came at last, and at the 1999 "IAA" Porsche celebrated the 911 Turbo's 25th anniversary with a turbocharged version of the Type 996. Once again, fans and journalists alike were delighted by its built-in advanced technology. The data sheet declared the power output to be 420 hp and the maximum torque 560 Newton-meters. With this high power and abundant torque on tap, acceleration was brilliant: from 0 to 100 kph (62 mph) took only 4.2 seconds. The new Turbo was faster than Porsche's GT3 and led the way at the top of the 911 model line. Despite the immense amount of available power, however, traction problems were unknown on the 911 Turbo because of its all-wheel drive, which was standard equipment. Engine power reached the front wheels as

Der Sechszylinder-Biturbo
leistete 420 PS
*The twin-turbo six-cylinder
engine developed 420 hp*

before through a viscous coupling, but no more than 40 percent of the available torque was diverted in this way in order to avoid drive-train influences on the car's handling. Close to the handling limit, the driver was assisted by Porsche Stability Management (PSM), which eased back the throttle or applied the brake at individual wheels.

The Type 996 was the first Turbo generation to be offered for sale with 5-speed Tiptronic S as an option. Customers accustomed to automatic transmission were finally able to choose the Porsche Turbo. The car's high torque made it necessary to develop a new automatic transmission selector, and at the same time the electronic control system was upgraded technically to state-of-the-art specification. Instead of five fixed shift points, the programs now allowed for the driver's individual style and preferences.

The engine was the outcome of a minor revolution: For the first time in The Turbo's history, the power source was a completely water-cooled six-cylinder horizontally opposed engine, but not the design used in the Carrera and Boxster models. As in the GT1 and GT3,

Prozent limitiert, um störende Einflüsse auf das Fahrverhalten zu vermeiden. In Grenzsituationen unter-
stützte den Fahrer überdies das Porsche Stability
Management (PSM) durch automatisches Gaswegnehmen oder durch Bremseingriff an einzelnen Rädern.

Als erste Turbo-Generation konnte der 996 auch mit
5-Gang-Tiptronic S erworben werden, so dass auch
für an Automatik gewöhnte Kunden die Turbo-lose
Zeit ein Ende hatte. Das hohe Drehmoment machte
eine Neuentwicklung der Automatikschaltung notwendig,
wobei auch die elektronische Getriebesteuerung auf
den neuesten Stand der Technik gebracht wurde. Statt
fünf festgelegter Programme konnten die Schaltpunkte
nun an die individuelle Fahrweise angepasst werden.

Der Motor war eine kleine Revolution: Erstmals in
der Turbo-Historie kam die Kraft aus einem komplett
wassergekühlten Sechszylinder-Boxer mit 3,6 Liter
Hubraum, der sich jedoch in seinem Aufbau von den
Carrera- und Boxster-Modellen unterschied. Wie beim
GT1 oder GT3 bildeten Motorgehäuse, Zylinderblöcke
und Zylinderköpfe separate Einheiten. Die vier oben-
liegenden Nockenwellen wurden über Rollenketten

the engine block, cylinder blocks and cylinder heads
were separate units. The four overhead camshafts were
driven by roller chains directly from the crankshaft.
To boost performance, enhance refinement and
minimize exhaust emissions, the engine was equipped
with variable inlet valve lift. This system, known as
"VarioCam Plus", also helped to keep fuel consumption
low. At 12.9 liters per 100 kilometers (18.2 US,
21.9 UK mpg), the total consumption according to
the EU test cycle was 18 percent below the figure
achieved by the previous model, and the exhaust
emissions were about 50 percent lower, so that the
new 911 Turbo easily outperformed the EU4 limits and
the American LEV standard.
The engine was supplied with combustion air by two
turbochargers, each with a charge-air intercooler.
Boost pressure was regulated according to demand
by an electronically controlled waste gate. When
peak torque was called for, absolute pressure in the
intake system could reach 1.85 bar, but this value
was gradually lowered as maximum engine speed was
approached. Digital Motor Electronics monitored the
ignition and fuel injection and repositioned the
electronic throttle according to the settings determined

unmittelbar von der Kurbelwelle angetrieben. Zur Verbesserung der Leistung, der Laufkultur und Abgasreinigung arbeitete der Motor mit einer Ventilhub-Umschaltung auf der Einlassseite. Das »VarioCam Plus« genannte System wirkte sich auch positiv auf den Verbrauch aus. Mit 12,9 Liter pro 100 Kilometer lag der Gesamtverbrauch nach EG-Norm um 18 Prozent niedriger als beim Vorgänger-Modell. Auch die Abgaswerte konnten um rund 50 Prozent gesenkt werden, wodurch der 911 Turbo problemlos die EU4-Grenzwerte und den amerikanischen LEV-Standard erfüllte. Die Aufladung des Motors erfolgte über zwei Turbolader mit je einem Ladeluftkühler. Der Ladedruck wurde über ein elektronisch gesteuertes »Wastegate«-Abblasventil von der Motronic bedarfsgerecht geregelt. Der Absolutdruck im Einlasssystem erreichte im Bereich des höchsten Drehmoments ein Maximum von 1,85 bar; bis zum Erreichen der Nenndrehzahl wurde der Wert kontinuierlich gesenkt. Die digitale Motorelektronik kontrollierte Zündung und Einspritzung und betätigte, entsprechend der Fahrdynamikregelung PSM per E-Gas die Drosselklappe. Für die Abgasreinigung waren zwei Metallkatalysatoren mit Stereo-Lambda-Sonden-Regelung verantwortlich.

Die markante Frontpartie des 996 Turbo sorgte für Überholprestige
The bold front-end styling of the 996 Turbo commanded respect in the overtaking lane

RECHTE SEITE: Designskizze des 911 Turbo Coupé (996), circa 1998
RIGHT PAGE: *Design sketch for the 911 Turbo Coupé (996), about 1998*

by the PSM dynamic regulating system. For exhaust emission control, two metal-monolith catalytic converters with a stereo lambda probe regulating system were provided.

In the design area the new Turbo demonstrated its personality and also set itself apart clearly from the Carrera. The typically wide Turbo fenders and the rear spoiler were not the whole story: in the front apron, three large cooling air intakes lined with dark material drew attention unmistakably to the Turbo in the mirror of the car in front. This was not merely power-play: the higher power output called for a radiator area about 50 percent larger than on the 911 Carrera. Exclusive to the Turbo were headlamps with bi-xenon bulbs that emitted a blue-tinged light. The rear side panels were restyled, and there were narrow slots in the widened rear fenders to supply air to the intercoolers. The extending rear wing was a completely new design, and a rear panel with air outlets similar to those first seen on the Porsche 959 emphasized the individual character of Porsche's new top model.

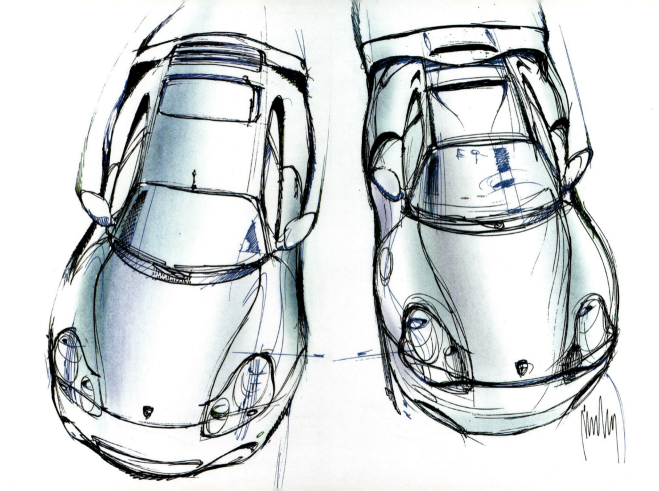

Beim Design zeigte der neue Turbo seine Persönlich-
keit in klarer Abgrenzung zum Carrera und ging weit
über die Turbo-typischen breiten Kotflügel und den
Heckspoiler hinaus. In der Frontschürze sorgten drei
große, dunkel verkleidete Kühlluftöffnungen für einen
markanten Auftritt im Rückspiegel, denn aufgrund der
höheren Motorleistung musste die Gesamtfläche der
Kühler gegenüber dem 911-Saugmotor um 50 Prozent
gesteigert werden. Die vorderen Scheinwerfer-Einheiten
wurden Turbo-exklusiv mit bläulich strahlenden Bi-
Xenon-Lampen bestückt. Auch die Fondseitenteile
wurden stilistisch neu gestaltet. Schmal geschnittene
Lufteinlasskanäle für die Ladeluftkühler prägten
die verbreiterten hinteren Kotflügel. Im Heckbereich
unterstrich außerdem ein völlig neu entwickelter
ausfahrbarer Flügel sowie eine Heckverkleidung mit
Luftaustrittsöffnungen à la 959 den eigenständigen
Auftritt des Porsche-Topmodells.

Insgesamt hatte die Aerodynamik einen weiteren
Sprung nach vorne gemacht: Mit einem cw von
0,31 übertraf der neue 911 Turbo seinen Vorgänger
um drei Punkte, was sich gleichermaßen positiv auf
Höchstgeschwindigkeit und Verbrauch auswirkte.

Das US-Modell des
911 Turbo Coupé war ab
Januar 2000 erhältlich
The US version of the 911
Turbo Coupe was available
from January 2000 on

LINKE SEITE: Das 911 Turbo
Coupé wurde im Windkanal
des EZW optimiert
LEFT PAGE: *The 911 Turbo
Coupé was optimized in the
EZW wind tunnel*

The aerodynamics made a quantum leap forward:
with a drag coefficient of $c_D = 0.31$ the new 911
Turbo outperformed its predecessor by three decimal
points. This development proved its worth in the
form of higher top speed and lower fuel consumption.
With a top speed of 305 kph (190 mph), the 911 Turbo
was now a well-established member of the elite
club of sports cars capable of exceeding 300 kph.
To permit excursions into this rarefied speed zone
without unnecessary risk, Porsche redesigned the
car's brake system. From now on, the 911 Turbo
was brought to a halt by four-piston monobloc fixed-
caliper disk brakes. At this time too, the Stuttgart-
based sports car manufacturer began to offer a
further option, the first carmaker in the world to do
so: the revolutionary Porsche Ceramic Composite
Brake (PCCB). Available on the 911 Turbo from August
2000 on, the composite ceramic brake disks had
involute cooling ducts molded into them, and set new
standards in initial response, resistance to fading,
weight saving and operating life.

Very soon after the press had been invited to drive the
new 911 Turbo in March 2000, its success potential

Löst Bewegung aus.
Selbst im Stillstand.

Der 911 Turbo.

Werbeanzeige für den
911 Turbo (2000)
*911 Turbo advertisement
(2000)*

RECHTS: Dr. Wolfgang
Porsche und der 911 Turbo
auf der IAA 2003
RIGHT: *Dr. Wolfgang Porsche
and the 911 Turbo at the
2003 German Motor Show*

Mit einer Höchstgeschwindigkeit von 305 km/h gehörte der 911 Turbo nun fest zum elitären Club der 300-Stundenkilometer-Sportwagen. Damit ein Ausflug in diese Geschwindigkeitsbereiche kein Sicherheitsrisiko darstellte, machte sich Porsche an die Überarbeitung der Bremsanlage. Serienmäßig verzögerte der 911 Turbo mit einer Vierkolben-Monobloc-Festsattelbremse. Optional bot der Stuttgarter Sportwagenhersteller noch ein revolutionäres Bremssystem an: die Porsche Ceramic Composite Brake (PCCB). Als weltweit erster Hersteller lieferte Porsche im 911 Turbo ab August 2000 eine Keramik-Verbundbremsscheibe mit Evolventen-Kühlkanal, die bei Kriterien wie Ansprechverhalten, Fadingstabilität, Gewicht und Lebensdauer neue Maßstäbe setzte.

Schon bald nach der Pressefahrvorstellung im März 2000 stand fest, dass der neue 911 Turbo ein Erfolgstyp werden würde. Fachjournalisten aus aller Welt bescheinigten ihm, neue Maßstäbe zu setzen und in der Summe seiner Eigenschaften die Spitze im internationalen Sportwagenbau zu markieren. Auch die Nachfrage übertraf alle Erwartungen: Schon im ersten Jahr seiner Produktion stockte Porsche die

Gelbsucht: Porsche Ceramic Composite Break PCCB
Yellow for safety: Porsche Ceramic Composite Brake (PCCB)

was obvious. Trade journalists from all over the world agreed that it set new standards and that the sum of its fine qualities put it at the head of the international sports-car field. Customer demand exceeded all expectations: even in the first year of production Porsche was obliged to increase planned output of this model from 2,500 to 4,000 cars. In a subsequent product offensive, Porsche went a step farther and increased the number of Turbo versions on offer. In the 2004 model year, customers were not only offered a power increase to 450 hp, but also a convertible body style. This was the first Turbo convertible to go on sale since 1987; by June 2005, more than 3,500 customers had chosen this model.

In May 2004, shortly before the new-generation 911 – the Type 997 – was due to appear, Porsche added the 911 Turbo S and the 911 Turbo S Convertible to its product program. The S versions had uprated engines and the PCCB ceramic disk brakes as standard equipment. Larger turbochargers and intercoolers, together with modified engine management electronics, raised the power output to 450 hp and the top speed to 307 kph (191 mph). The German car

Das 911 Turbo Cabriolet
erweiterte das Verkaufs-
programm ab dem Herbst
2003
*Left: The 911 Turbo Cabrio-
let was added to the model
program in the fall of 2003*

LINKE SEITE: Vom 911 Turbo
Coupé (996) entstanden
22.062 Einheiten
LEFT PAGE: *Porsche built
22,062 Type 996 Turbo
Coupes*

geplante Stückzahl von 2.500 auf 4.000 Einheiten auf. Im Rahmen der Produktoffensive erweiterte Porsche das Modellangebot auch bei den Turbo-Varianten. Für das Modelljahr 2004 offerierte Porsche nicht nur eine Leistungssteigerung auf 450 PS, sondern auch eine Cabrio-Variante des 911 Turbo. Erstmals seit 1987 war somit wieder ein Turbo Cabriolet erhältlich, das bis Juni 2005 über 3.500 Abnehmer fand.

Im Mai 2004 – die Einführung der neuen Elfergeneration 997 stand vor der Tür – erweiterte Porsche die Produktpalette um die Typen 911 Turbo S und 911 Turbo S Cabriolet. Charakteristisch für die »S«-Varianten waren das gesteigerte Leistungspotenzial des Motors sowie die serienmäßige Keramikbremsanlage PCCB. Größere Turbolader und Ladeluftkühlung sowie eine überarbeitete Motorelektronik sorgten für 450 PS und 307 km/h Spitze. Der Preis von 142.250 Euro für das Coupé und 152.225 Euro für das Cabriolet wurde von der »AutoBild« als Schnäppchen bezeichnet, denn in den 13.572 Euro Aufpreis gegenüber dem normalen Turbo waren neben 30 Mehr-PS auch eine serienmäßige Keramikbremse und ein CD-Wechsler enthalten.

magazine "AutoBild" described the prices of 142,250 Euro charged for the Coupe and 152,225 Euro for the Convertible as a "steal": the additional 13,572 Euro compared with the regular Turbo purchased 30 more horsepower, the ceramic-disk brake system and a CD changer.

KLASSIK UND MODERNE –
DER 911 TURBO IN DER SECHSTEN GENERATION
CLASSIC AND MODERN –
THE SIXTH-GENERATION 911 TURBO

KLASSIK UND MODERNE –
DER 911 TURBO IN DER SECHSTEN GENERATION
CLASSIC AND MODERN –
THE SIXTH-GENERATION 911 TURBO

Eine weitere Evolutionsstufe der 911-Baureihe konnte ab Juli 2004 in den 85 deutschen Porsche-Zentren besichtigt werden. Die intern als 997 bezeichnete Typenreihe wurde zunächst in zwei Leistungsvarianten mit unterschiedlichen Hubräumen angeboten: Der 911 Carrera als Basisvariante mit 3,6-Liter Hubraum und einer Leistung von 325 PS und der 911 Carrera S mit 3,8-Liter-Hubraum und einer Leistung von 355 PS. In den beiden Coupés, die stilistisch die klassische 911 Linie fortsetzten, erschloss sich den Fahrern damit eine neue Qualität an Fahrdynamik.

Das Design der Generation 997 war eine konsequente Fortsetzung der bisherigen Modellreihe. Die breitere Spur und die stärkere Taille ließen den Sportwagen kraftvoll und athletisch auf der Straße stehen – und

Porsche 911 Turbo
»Typ 997« (Modelljahr 2006)
*Type 997 Porsche 911 Turbo
(2006 model year)*

In July 2004, the 85 German Porsche Centers began to display a further evolutionary version of the 911 model line. Known internally as the 997, it was available at first with two engine sizes and power outputs. The 911 Carrera was the basic version, with a 325-horsepower 3.6-liter engine. The 911 Carrera S had the larger 3.8-liter engine rated at 355 hp. Both retained the classic 911 Coupe body outline but offered drivers a new quality of road dynamics.

The 997 model family was a systematic continuation of the previous model line. A wider track and a more emphatic waistline gave this sports car a strong, athletic stance – and performance to match. Other striking features of the 997 design were classic oval headlamps with separate foglamps in the nose

erst recht fahren. Weitere markante Merkmale des 997-Designs waren die klassischen Oval-Scheinwerfer mit separaten Zusatzscheinwerfern im Bugteil, stärker betonte Kotflügel, Doppelarm-Außenspiegel, der aerodynamisch optimierte Heckspoiler und die markante Fugenoptik insbesondere am Heckteil. Die neue Figur des Porsche 911 bot gleichzeitig auch aerodynamische Vorteile und verbesserte den Luftwiderstands-Beiwert auf $c_w = 0{,}28$.

Auf die 911 Carrera-Modelle mit Saugmotor folgte im Februar 2006 die sechste Generation des Turbo. Als Spitzenmodell der Elfer-Baureihe verfügte der 997 Turbo als erstes Serienautomobil mit Benzinmotor über einen Turbolader mit variabler Turbinengeometrie (VTG). Der 911 Turbo der Typenreihe 997 leistete jetzt 480 PS bei 6.000 Umdrehungen pro Minute, 60 PS mehr als sein Vorgänger. Die spezifische Leistung des 3,6-Liter Boxermotors kletterte damit auf die neue Höchstmarke von 133 PS pro Liter Hubraum. Das Nenndrehmoment war von 560 auf 620 Newtonmeter gestiegen. Gleichzeitig wurde das Drehzahlband, bei dem diese Kraft zur Verfügung stand, erweitert. Während das maximale Drehmoment

Zu Walter Röhrls Aufgaben zählte die Fahrwerksabstimmung des 911 Turbo *Suspension tuning on the Type 997 Turbo was a task entrusted to star driver Walter Röhrl*

section of the body, double-arm outside mirror mounts, aerodynamically optimized rear spoilers and a bold pattern of joint lines, especially at the rear of the body. These new styling measures also improved the Porsche 911's aerodynamics; drag coefficient cD was now 0.28.

The new 911 Carrera models with naturally aspirated engine were followed in February 2006 by the sixth-generation Turbo. As the top model in this line, the 997 Turbo was the first series-production car with gasoline engine to have a turbocharger with variable turbine geometry (VTG). This new 911 Turbo had a power output of 480 hp at 6000 rpm – 60 hp more than the previous model. The specific output of the 3.6-liter flat-six engine went up to a new peak value of 133 hp per liter. Maximum torque also rose, from 560 to 620 Newton-meters, and was at the driver's command over a greater engine-speed range: between 1950 and 5000 rpm instead of 2700 to 4600 rpm on the previous model.

These improvements were reflected in the car's performance: for the standing-start sprint from 0 to 100 kph (62 mph) the turbocharged Type

Das Porsche Traction
Management (PTM)
sorgte für die optimale
Kraftverteilung
*Porsche Traction Manage-
ment (PTM) ensures the best
possible torque split*

beim Vorgängermodell zwischen 2.700 und 4.600 Umdrehungen pro Minute anstand, ließ es sich nun im Bereich zwischen 1.950 und 5.000 Touren abrufen.

Diese Verbesserungen ließen sich auch an den Fahrleistungen ablesen: Für den Standardsprint von 0 auf 100 km/h benötigte der Turbo-aufgeladene 997 mit Sechsgang-Schaltgetriebe 3,9 Sekunden, das Coupé erreichte die 200-Stundenkilometer-Marke in 12,8 Sekunden. Lediglich 3,8 Sekunden vergingen, bis der stärkste Serien-Elfer aller Zeiten im fünften Gang von Tempo 80 auf 120 km/h beschleunigt hatte. Trotz der Mehrleistung konnten die Porsche-Entwickler den durchschnittlichen Kraftstoffverbrauch um ein Zehntel auf 12,8 Liter pro 100 Kilometer senken. Noch beeindruckender waren die Werte des 911 Turbo mit dem optional verfügbaren Automatikgetriebe Tiptronic S. Dank einer optimierten Abstimmung spurtete das Fahrzeug in nur 3,7 Sekunden auf Hundert und erreichte bereits nach 12,2 Sekunden Tempo 200. Auch bei der Elastizität hat der Turbo mit Automatikgetriebe die Nase vorn: Im vorletzten Gang beschleunigte er in 3,5 Sekunden von 80 auf 120 km/h. Der Kraftstoffverbrauch sank bei der Tiptronic S-Variante

Werbeanzeige für den 911 Turbo (2006)
Advertisement for the 911 Turbo dating 2006

Destined for an art museum or a science museum?

The new 911 Turbo

im Vergleich zum Vorgänger um 0,3 Liter und betrug nach EU-Norm 13,6 Liter. Die Höchstgeschwindigkeit für beide Getriebe-Varianten lag bei 310 km/h.

Mit der erstmals angebotenen Sonderausstattung »Sport Chrono Paket Turbo« ließ sich die Elastizität des Fahrzeugs sogar noch verbessern. Betätigte der Fahrer die »Sporttaste« neben dem Schalthebel, wurde bei voller Beschleunigung ein kurzzeitiger »Overboost« aktiviert. Dabei wurde der Ladedruck im mittleren Drehzahlbereich bis zu zehn Sekunden lang um 0,2 bar angehoben, und das Drehmoment stieg um 60 auf 680 Newtonmeter. Die Zeit für die Zwischen-beschleunigung von 80 auf 120 km/h verkürzte sich damit beim handgeschalteten 911 Turbo um 0,3 auf 3,5 Sekunden.

Verantwortlich für diese Fahrleistungen waren die erstmals beim Ottomotor eingesetzten Abgasturbo-lader mit variabler Turbinengeometrie. Kernelemente dieser Technologie waren verstellbare Leitschaufeln, die den Abgasstrom des Motors variabel und gezielt auf das Turbinenrad des Abgasturboladers leiteten. Das Prinzip der variablen Turbinengeometrie verband

Das »Sport Chrono Paket Turbo« ermöglichte per Knopfdruck einen »Overboost«
The "Sport Chrono Paket Turbo" switches to overboost when a button is pressed

997 Coupe with six-speed stick shift needed only 3.9 seconds, and passed the 200 kph (124 mph) mark in 12.8 seconds. The most powerful 911 model of all time was flexible too, needing only 3.8 seconds to accelerate from 80 to 120 kph (50 to 75 mph) in fifth gear. Yet with all this additional performance on call, Porsche's engineers were able to cut the average fuel consumption by one-tenth, to 12.8 liters per 100 kilometers (18.4 US, 22.1 UK mpg). The figures for the 911 Turbo with the optional Tiptronic S automatic transmission were even more impressive. Thanks to optimized settings, this version of the car needed only 3.7 seconds to reach 100 kph (62 mph) from a standstill, and 12.2 seconds to pass the 200 kph (124 mph) mark. The Turbo's flexibility with automatic transmission was also better than its manual-shift counterpart; with the selector in the second-highest gear position, acceleration from 80 to 120 kph (50 to 75 mph) took only 3.5 seconds. The Tiptronic S version's fuel consumption by the standard EU test method was 13.6 liters per 100 km (17.3 US, 20.8 UK mpg), 0.3 litre/100 km (0.4 US/0.3 UK mpg) better than the previous model. Top speed was 310 kph (193 mph) with either transmission.

die Vorteile von kleinen und großen Abgasturboladern und führte insbesondere bei niedrigen Drehzahlen zu einer spürbaren Verbesserung der Elastizität und Beschleunigung.

Um die vorhandene Kraft optimal auf die Straße zu übertragen, verfügte die sechste Generation des 911 Turbo über einen neu entwickelten Allradantrieb mit elektronisch gesteuerter Lamellenkupplung. Das Porsche Traction Management (PTM) sorgte für eine variable Kraftverteilung auf beide Antriebsachsen. Abhängig vom Fahrzustand ermittelte die Allradelektronik kontinuierlich die jeweils optimale Momentverteilung und garantierte so den bestmöglichen Antrieb. In der Praxis bedeutete dies: Hohe Agilität auf engen Landstraßen, herausragende Traktion bei Nässe und Schnee sowie optimale Fahrsicherheit auch im Hochgeschwindigkeitsbereich. Das Porsche Traction Management im neuen 911 Turbo gehörte mit diesen Eigenschaften zu den leistungsfähigsten und gleichzeitig leichtesten Allrad-Systemen auf dem Markt.

Wie üblich beim Porsche 911 Turbo, stand den hohen Fahrleistungen ein adäquates Bremssystem gegen-

LINKE SEITE:
Serienmäßig: das aktive Dämpfungssystem Porsche Active Suspension Management (PASM)
LEFT PAGE: On all cars: Porsche Active Suspension Management (PASM)

Weltneuheit: Abgas-Turbolader mit variabler Turbinengeometrie (VTG)
World premiere: turbocharger with variable turbine geometry (VTG)

The "Sport Chrono Turbo" package, offered as an optional extra for the first time, improved the car's flexibility still further. If the driver pressed the "Sport" button next to the gear shift and then accelerated as hard as possible, the engine switched to "overboost" for a short time. Boost pressure was raised by 0.2 bar for up to ten seconds in the medium engine-speed range, so that torque went up by 60 to 680 Newton-meters. This cut the time needed for the manual-shift 911 Turbo to accelerate from 80 to 120 kph (50 to 75 mph) by 0.3 of a second, to only 3.5 seconds.

Part of the secret of such high performance was the turbocharger with variable turbine geometry (VTG), used here for the first time on a spark-ignition engine. The key elements of this device are the adjustable vanes that direct the exhaust gas from the engine onto the turbine wheel at the most favorable angle. The VTG principle combined the advantages of small and large turbochargers and resulted in a distinct improvement in flexibility and acceleration, especially at low engine speeds.

LINKE SEITE: Der ausfahr-
bare und neu geformte
Spaltflügel über der Motor-
haube sorgte für Abtrieb
LEFT PAGE: *The reshaped
wing on the engine cover
can be extended, and
generates downthrust*

Mit 1.585 Kilogramm war
der neue Turbo um fünf
Kilogramm leichter als sein
Vorgänger
*At 1,585 kilograms
(3494 lbs) the new Turbo
was five kilograms (11 lbs)
lighter than the previous
model*

über. Zum Einsatz kamen Monobloc-Festsattelbrem-sen mit sechs Kolben an der Vorderachse und vier Kolben an der Hinterachse.

Der Durchmesser der innenbelüfteten und gelochten Bremsscheiben wurde im Vergleich zum Typ 996 an der Vorder- und Hinterachse um 20 Millimeter auf 350 Millimeter vergrößert. Als Option bot Porsche darüber hinaus die weiterentwickelte Keramikbrems-anlage PCCB (Porsche Ceramic Composite Brake) an. Vorteile des Hightech-Materials waren ein um 17 Kilo-gramm geringeres Gewicht gegenüber der Serien-bremsanlage, sehr hohe Fadingstabilität aufgrund kon-stanter Reibwerte und absolute Korrosionssicherheit. 380 Millimeter betrug nun der Durchmesser an der Vorderachse und 350 Millimeter an der Hinterachse.

Charakteristisches Designmerkmal dieses 911 Turbo war das neu geformte Bugteil mit seinen markanten, straff ausmodellierten Kühllufteinlässen. In Verbindung mit den serienmäßigen ovalen Bi-Xenon-Scheinwerfern prägten sie sein unverwechselbares Gesicht. Abgerun-det wurde die harmonische Frontansicht von den weit außen und tief stehenden Nebelscheinwerfern sowie den neuen LED-Blinkleuchten, die in den seitlichen

Das 19-Zoll Turbo Rad zählte zur Serienausstattung
19-inch Turbo wheels were standard equipment

RECHTE SEITE: Hohe Fahr-stabilität und berechen-bare Reaktionen auch bei Höchstgeschwindigkeit
RIGHT PAGE: *High dynamic stability and predictable reactions even at very high speeds*

To get all this power onto the road effectively, a new all-wheel-drive system with an electronically controlled multi-plate clutch was developed for the sixth-generation 911 Turbo. Porsche Traction Management (PTM) distributed the power between the axles. The all-wheel-drive electronics monitored driving conditions continuously and determined how much torque should be supplied to each axle for the best possible traction. The practical advantages: excellent agility on twisting country roads, outstanding traction on wet or snow-covered roads and optimal road safety even at very high speeds. Porsche Traction Management for the new 911 Turbo was among the top-performing all-wheel-drive systems on the market, and also among the lightest in weight.

The Porsche 911 Turbo would not be such a supreme car unless its high performance were matched by an equally effective brake system. Monobloc fixed-caliper disk brakes were specified, with six pistons at the front wheels and four at the rear. Compared with the Type 996, the perforated and ventilated brake disks were increased in diameter by 20 millimeters (0.8 in) to 350 millimeters (13.8 in). As an option, Porsche

Lufteinlässen des Bugteils positioniert waren. Von hinten betrachtet erschien der Turbo ebenfalls kraftvoller als bisher. Dazu trug vor allem die gegenüber dem Vorgängermodell um insgesamt 22 Millimeter verbreiterte Heckpartie bei, an die der neu geformte Spaltflügel angepasst wurde. Dieser neigte sich an den Flanken nun leicht nach unten und schmiegte sich so an die Form der hinteren Kotflügel an. Die seitlichen Lufteinlässe hinter den Türen wurden ebenfalls neu gestaltet und ermöglichten zusammen mit den neuen Luftkanälen eine effizientere Kühlluftzufuhr zu den Ladeluftkühlern.

Der neue 911 Turbo besaß gegenüber dem Vorgängermodell ein komplett neu gestaltetes Interieur mit serienmäßiger Lederausstattung, das auf der 911 Carrera-Generation 997 basierte. Die Instrumente mit aluminiumfarbenen Zifferblättern entsprachen dem charakteristischen 911-Design mit Turbo-Schriftzug im Drehzahlmesser. Für eine größere Leuchtkraft der Zifferblätter bei Nacht wurden weiße Leuchtdioden eingesetzt. Im Display des mittleren Rundinstrumentes wurde der Ladedruck erstmals auch als Balkendiagramm angezeigt. Zum neuen Innenraum-Design gehörte auch ein Schalthebel im speziellen Turbo-Look.

Die Aerodynamik stimmte auch beim neuen Maßanzug des 911 Turbo: c_w = 0,31
The 911 Turbo's new outer skin was aerodynamically efficient, with a drag coefficient (cD) of 0.31

RECHTE SEITE: Hochwertige Serienausstattung im Innenraum
RIGHT PAGE: *High-value interior equipment and trim*

offered customers a further developed version of its PCCB (Porsche Ceramic Composite Brake) ceramic-disk brake system. Advantages of this hi-tech disk material: 17 kilograms (37.5 lbs) less weight than the standard brake system, constant friction values for very high resistance to fading and absolute freedom from corrosion. These disks had a diameter of 380 mm (15 in) at the front and 350 mm (13.8 in) at the rear.

A characteristic design feature of this 911 Turbo was the restyled nose section of the body with its boldly shaped cooling air intakes. Together with the standard oval bi-xenon headlamps, the front end was harmonious and unmistakable in appearance, and included foglamps mounted low down and wide apart and new LED flashers in the side air intakes. Seen from the rear, the Turbo looked more potent than the previous model, mainly because the rear of the body was 22 millimeters (0.9 in) wider than before, with a restyled wing in two sections, inclined slightly down at the ends. The air intakes behind the doors were also restyled and, together with new ducts, supply cooling air more effectively to the charge air intercoolers.

Wie das Vorgängermodell war auch dieser 911 Turbo serienmäßig mit dem Porsche Communication Management (PCM) einschließlich DVD-Navigationsmodul ausgerüstet. Zu den weiteren serienmäßigen Ausstat-

Porsche 911 Turbo (Modelljahr 2009)
Porsche 911 Turbo (2009 model year)

Compared with the previous model, the interior of the new 911 Turbo was completely redesigned, with leather upholstery and trim based on the 997-generation 911 Carrera as part of the standard specification. With their aluminum-colored dials, the instruments were of characteristic 911 design, but with Turbo lettering on the rev counter. White light-emitting diodes were used to make the instruments more easily legible after dark. The central circular instrument dial included for the first time a turbocharger boost pressure display in the form of a bar graph. The new interior design also featured a Turbo-look gear lever.

Like the previous model, this 911 Turbo was supplied with Porsche Communication Management (PCM) as standard equipment, including a DVD navigation module. Other standard items included automatic anti-glare mirrors and an anti-theft alarm with radar sensors that monitored the car's interior and had contacts on the body. Like all the other cars in the latest 911 program, this top model offered its occupants a very high standard of passive safety. There were six airbags altogether, including full-size airbags for the driver and front passenger, two head-

tungsdetails zählten unter anderem automatisch ab-
blendende Rückspiegel und eine Diebstahlwarnanlage,
die per Radarsensoren sowohl den Innenraum als auch
kontaktgesteuert die Außenhaut überwacht. Wie die
gesamte 911 Baureihe bot auch das Spitzenmodell
eine sehr hohe passive Sicherheit. Zu den insgesamt
sechs Airbags gehörten neben dem Fullsize-Airbag für
Fahrer- und Beifahrer auch die beiden Kopfairbags in
den Seitenfensterbrüstungen, die bei einem Seitenauf-
prall simultan mit den Thorax-Airbags in den Vorder-
sitzlehnen aktiviert und von Porsche weltweit erstmals
eingesetzt wurden.

Leistungshungrigen Frischluftenthusiasten wurde
2007 auf der IAA eine neue Generation des 911 Turbo
Cabriolets präsentiert. Ein technischer Höhepunkt des
offenen Turbo-Elfers war die Synthese aus geringem
Gewicht und hoher Karosserie-Steifigkeit sowie aus
kompakten Abmessungen und maßgeschneiderter
Innenraum-Ergonomie. Dank des intelligenten Leicht-
baus lag die für Fahrpräzision und Qualitätseindruck
wesentliche Torsionssteifigkeit über 9.000 Newtonmeter pro Grad und damit im internationalen Spitzen-
feld bei offenen Fahrzeugen.

480 PS standen beim
911 Turbo Cabriolet
lediglich 1.655 Kilogramm
Leergewicht gegenüber
The 911 Turbo Convertible's
480-horsepower engine
had an easy task with a car
weighing only 1,655 kilo-
grams (3,650 lbs)

level airbags in the side window surrounds and –
capable of operating in tandem with them – thorax
airbags in the front seat backs; Porsche was the first
manufacturer inn the world to provide these.

Drivers who liked a dash of fresh air with their
power cocktail were offered a new-generation
911 Turbo convertible at the 2007 German Motor
Show. A technical highspot of the open 911 Turbo
was its brilliant combination of low weight and high
body rigidity, as well as compact dimensions and
tailormade interior ergonomics. Thanks to intelligent
weight-saving design, the torsional rigidity that is so
important for precision steering and a sense of quality
was increased to more than 9,000 Newton-meters,
among the highest figures recorded by an open car
anywhere in the world.

Generationenvertrag: Porsche 911 Turbo 3.3 und 911 Turbo (997)
Linking the generations: Porsche 911 Turbo 3.3 and 911 Turbo (997)

**DER NEUE PORSCHE 911 TURBO – DER SPARSAMSTE
UND KRAFTVOLLSTE TOP-ELFER ALLER ZEITEN**
THE NEW PORSCHE 911 TURBO – THE MOST POWERFUL
AND ECONOMICAL TOP MODEL THE 911 PROGRAM
HAS EVER HAD

DER NEUE PORSCHE 911 TURBO – DER SPARSAMSTE UND KRAFTVOLLSTE TOP-ELFER ALLER ZEITEN
THE NEW PORSCHE 911 TURBO – THE MOST POWERFUL AND ECONOMICAL TOP MODEL THE 911 PROGRAM HAS EVER HAD

Mit dem neuen 911 Turbo, der im September 2009 auf der IAA in Frankfurt Weltpremiere feierte, setzte Porsche einmal mehr ein Zeichen im Segment der Hochleistungssportwagen: Die Entwicklung zu mehr Effizienz bei weniger Emissionen, zu mehr Fahrdynamik bei weniger Gewicht, ist zukunftsweisend. Konkret verbraucht das neue Topmodell der Seriensportwagen aus Zuffenhausen bis zu 16 Prozent weniger Kraftstoff, entwickelt 20 PS mehr Leistung, 30 Nm mehr Drehmoment und legt um bis zu acht Prozent verkürzte Beschleunigungszeiten bei einem Mindergewicht von bis zu 25 Kilogramm vor – vom Mehr an Fahrdynamik ganz zu schweigen. Damit setzt sich der neue Top-Elfer aus Zuffenhausen vor allem in puncto Effizienz und Spurtstärke noch deutlicher als bisher von seinen Wettbewerbern ab.

Offene Versuchung:
911 Turbo Cabriolet
(Modelljahr 2010)
An open temptation: 911 Turbo Convertible (2010 model year)

LINKE SEITE: Die neueste Generation des 911 Turbo
LEFT PAGE: *The latest 911 Turbo generation*

In September 2009, when the latest 911 Turbo was launched at the German "IAA" Motor Show in Frankfurt, Porsche once again reached a milestone in the high-performance sports car segment: greater efficiency, lower emissions, even more dynamic road behavior and lower weight – a forward-looking development trend. In figures: The Zuffenhausen-based manufacturer's new top model consumes up to 16 percent less fuel, delivers 20 additional horsepower and 30 Newton-meters more torque, accelerates up to eight percent faster and has shed up to 25 kilograms (55 lbs) in weight. More than ever before, the new 911 Turbo sets itself apart from its competitors in efficiency and vivid, dynamic performance.

Herzstück und Glanzlicht des neuen Porsche Turbo ist der neue Motor mit nunmehr 3,8 statt 3,6 Litern Hubraum. Das erstmals in der 35-jährigen 911 Turbo-Typengeschichte von Grund auf neu konstruierte Triebwerk verfügt über Benzindirekteinspritzung, eine effizienzsteigernde Expansionssauganlage und die Porsche-exklusiven Turbolader mit variabler Turbinengeometrie (VTG) für Benzinmotoren. Damit steigt im Vergleich zum Vorgänger nicht nur die Leistung um 20 PS auf 500 PS (368 kW), sondern auch das maximale Drehmoment um 30 Nm auf 650 Nm.

Der 911 Turbo ist, wie bisher, serienmäßig mit einem Sechsgang-Schaltgetriebe ausgestattet. Als Option kann der Turbomotor erstmals mit einem Siebengang-Porsche-Doppelkupplungsgetriebe (PDK) kombiniert werden, das im Gegensatz zur Tiptronic S im Vorgänger auch mit Quersperre erhältlich ist. Es ist eine Weiterentwicklung des PDK aus den 911 Carrera-Sportwagen mit verstärkten Komponenten. Die Kombination aus PDK, Benzindirekteinspritzung und Turboaufladung ermöglicht ein neues Niveau an Effizienz, Agilität, Ansprechverhalten und Fahrleistungen.

Je nach Fahrzeugkonfiguration begnügt sich das neue Topmodell mit 11,4 bis 11,7 l/100 km (EU5-Norm) *Depending on the car's configuration, the new top model consumes no more than 11.4 to 11.7 liters of fuel per 100 kilometers (20.1–20.6 US, 24.1–24.8 UK mpg) and complies with the EU5 emission limits*

The central element and possibly the most outstanding feature of the new Porsche Turbo is the new engine, now with a displacement of 3.8 instead of 3.6 liters. It is a completely new design, the first in the 35-year history of the 911 Turbo models, with direct gasoline injection, an expansion air intake system to boost efficiency and turbochargers with variable turbine geometry (VTG), a Porsche exclusive for spark-ignition engines. Compared with the previous model, power output is up by 20 hp to 500 hp (368 kW), and maximum torque is now 30 Nm higher at 650 Nm.

As before, a six-speed stick-shift gearbox is standard equipment for the 911 Turbo. For the first time, however, the turbocharged engine can be combined as an option with a seven-speed Porsche double-clutch (PDK) gearbox. In contrast to the Tiptronic S automatic transmission in the previous model, this is available with a lateral differential lock. It is a version of the PDK developed from the 911 Carrera sports car, but with uprated components. The combination of PDK, direct gasoline injection and turbocharging achieves a new level of efficiency, agility, spontaneous response and high performance.

Der neue 911 Turbo
gilt als der sparsamste,
gleichzeitig aber
auch spurtschnellste
Hochleistungssportwagen
seiner Klasse
*The new 911 Turbo can
claim to be the most
economical high-
performance sports
car in its class, and is
also unbeatable when
accelerating*

Mit dem optionalen »Sport Chrono Paket Turbo«, das als Neuheit dynamische Motorlager umfasst, setzt der Top-Elfer auf seine sportlichen Bestleistungen noch eins drauf: Durch die integrierte Overboost-Funktion steigt das maximale Drehmoment um 50 auf 700 Nm. Damit sind nochmals schnellere Beschleunigungs-zeiten möglich – auch in Verbindung mit dem Schaltge-triebe. So gelingt der Spurt von Null auf 100 km/h mit gedrückter Sport-Taste in nur 3,6 Sekunden (Cabriolet 3,7 s) und in Kombination mit PDK, gedrückter Sport Plus-Taste und aktivierter Launch Control für bestmög-liche Anfahrbeschleunigung sogar in nur 3,4 Sekunden (Cabriolet 3,5 s). Von Null auf 200 km/h werden in diesem Modus nur 11,3 Sekunden benötigt (Cabriolet 11,8 s), die Höchstgeschwindigkeit beträgt 312 km/h.

Zusätzlich aktiviert die Sport Plus-Taste beim PDK die Schaltstrategie Rennstrecke mit kürzestmöglichen Schaltzeiten und optimalen Schaltpunkten beim Hoch- und Runterschalten. Zur weiteren Verbesse-rung sowohl der Fahrdynamik als auch des Fahr- und Schwingungskomforts besitzt das »Sport Chrono Paket Turbo« zusätzlich dynamische Motorlager. Diese verändern in Abhängigkeit der jeweiligen Fahrsitua-

Der 911 Turbo ist optional mit Porsche-Doppelkupp-lungsgetriebe erhältlich
The Porsche double-clutch transmission is an optional extra for the 911 Turbo

With the optional "Sport Chrono Turbo" package, which includes dynamic engine mounts as a new feature, the top 911 model exceeds all the performance records set up by earlier versions. The integral overboost function increases maximum torque by 50 Nm to 700 Nm. This means even faster acceleration, for the manual-shift version too. When the Sport button is pressed, 100 kph (62 mph) comes up from a standing start in only 3.6 seconds (Convertible: 3.7 seconds). With PDK, the Sport button pressed in and Launch Control activated, this acceleration figure can be cut to only 3.4 seconds (Convertible: 3.5 seconds). From 0 to 200 kph (124 mph) in this mode takes only 11.3 seconds (Convertible: 11.8 seconds). Top speed is 312 kph (194 mph).

The Sport Plus button also selects the racetrack gear-shift strategy at the PDK, for the shortest possible shift times and optimal up- and downshift points. The dynamic engine mounts in the Sport Chrono Turbo package improve refinement still more: they vary their stiffness and damping effect as the driving situation changes, and greatly reduce the amount of vibration

tion ihre Steifigkeit und Dämpfung. Dabei wird die Übertragung der Schwingungen und Vibrationen des gesamten Antriebsaggregats und insbesondere des Motors auf die Karosserie deutlich minimiert.

Die Alleinstellung in seinem Marktsegment sichert dem neuen Porsche Turbo sein um bis zu 16 Prozent geringerer Verbrauch, sogar nach der strengeren EU5-Norm. So gelang es, den Normverbrauch des 911 Turbo mit PDK gegenüber dem Vorgängermodell mit Tiptronic S um 2,2 auf 11,4 Liter pro 100 Kilometer zu senken. Im Überlandverkehr lassen sich sowohl Coupé als auch Cabriolet dank des optimal schaltenden PDK und verlustarmer Kraftübertragung problemlos unter zehn Liter pro 100 Kilometer bewegen (Außerstädtisch nach EU5-Norm: Coupé 8,1 l/100, Cabriolet 8,2 l/100 km). Noch deutlicher verbessern sich in der Gesamtbilanz die CO_2-Emissionen, die durch die Umstellung von Wandlerautomatik auf Doppelkupplungsgetriebe um knapp 18 Prozent sinken. Auch mit Schaltgetriebe liegen die Emissionsvorteile bei rund elf Prozent. Nahm der 911 Turbo schon bisher die Spitzenposition in der Disziplin Effizienz ein, vergrößert sich der Abstand im Wettbe

Der neue 911 Turbo wirkt noch kraftvoller und muskulöser
The new 911 Turbo is even more powerful and muscular

transmitted to the body, by the engine in particular and the drive train.

The factor that makes the Porsche Turbo unique in its market segment, however, is the reduction of up to 16 percent in fuel consumption – even though it complies with the new, tougher EU 5 emissions limits. The standard test-cycle consumption of the latest 911 Turbo with Porsche double-clutch transmission is 11.4 liters per 100 kilometers (20.6 US, 24.8 UK mpg), lower by 2.2 l/100 km (3.3 US, 4.0 UK mpg) than the previous car with Tiptronic S. On overland journeys both the Coupe and the Convertible, thanks to the PDK's optimal gear shifts and minimum losses in the driveline, can easily better 10 l/100 km (23.5 US, 28.2 UK mpg); the figures recorded in the extra-urban test in accordance with EU5 exhaust emission limits are 8.1 l/100 km (29.0 US, 34.9 UK mpg) for the Coupe and 8.2 l/100 km (28.7 US, 34.5 UK mpg) for the Convertible. Overall CO_2 emissions have improved even more dramatically: the change from conventional automatic to PDK double-clutch transmission has cut them by nearly 18 percent, and by about 11 percent on cars with a

werb jetzt nochmals drastisch. Als einziges Fahrzeug in seinem Marktsegment unterschreitet der Porsche 911 Turbo die Verbrauchsgrenzwerte der »Gas Guzzler Tax« in den USA, die verbrauchsintensive Fahrzeuge mit einer Zusatzsteuer belegt.

Die weiter verbesserten Fahrleistungen des neuen 911 Turbo gehen mit noch exzellenterer Fahrdynamik Hand in Hand. Die fahrdynamische Weiterentwicklung des aktiven Allradantriebes PTM und des Porsche Stability Managements PSM wird unterstützt durch das neue, optional erhältliche Porsche Torque Vectoring (PTV). Es beinhaltet ein mechanisches Hinterachssperrdifferenzial und erhöht durch gezielte Bremseneingriffe am kurveninneren Hinterrad die Agilität bei gleichzeitig reduzierter Untersteuer-Neigung. Dadurch werden Lenkpräzision sowie Kurvenstabilität gesteigert und höhere Kurvengeschwindigkeiten ermöglicht. Das PTM ist fahrdynamischer abgestimmt, Wechsel in der Momentenverteilung zwischen Vorder- und Hinterachse laufen sanfter ab. Für den Fahrer macht sich dies in einem sehr ausgeglichenen, berechenbaren Fahrverhalten bemerkbar.

Die Silhouette des 911 Turbo findet in den neuen LED-Heckleuchten einen markanten Abschluss
An eye-catching conclusion: the 911 Turbo's new LED rear lights

LINKE SEITE: Der 911 Turbo ist das alltags- und langstreckentaugliche Topmodell der Serien-Elfer
LEFT PAGE: *The 911 Turbo, the top model in the 911 program, is equally suitable as day-to-day transport or for long journeys*

manual-shift gearbox. The Porsche 911 Turbo has always been up among the leaders in efficiency, but now it has left its competitors well and truly behind. It is the only car in its segment of the market to outperform the fuel consumption limit imposed by the "Gas Guzzler Tax" in the USA, a penalty imposed on excessively thirsty cars.

Not only is the new 911 Turbo a top performer: it's more dynamic than ever on the road. PTM active all-wheel drive and Porsche Stability Management PSM have both been revised for more dynamic response, and can now be assisted by a new option: Porsche Torque Vectoring (PTV). This uses a mechanical rear-axle differential lock and controlled brake applications at the inside rear wheel when cornering, and makes the car more agile as well as minimizing any tendency to understeer. Steering precision and stability when cornering both benefit, and higher cornering speeds are possible. PTM now has more dynamic settings, and changes in torque distribution between the front and rear axles take place more smoothly. The driver is aware of these improvements as extremely well-balanced, predictable road behavior.

Die neue 911 Turbo-
Generation ist an Design-
Innovationen im Front-
und Heckbereich sowie
der neuen Lichttechnik
mit LED zu erkennen
*The latest 911 Turbo
generation can be identified
by design innovations at the
front and rear, and the new
LED lighting technology*

Das PTM kommuniziert im neuen 911 Turbo mit dem Porsche Stability Management, das ebenfalls zur Serienausstattung gehört. Mit dem Porsche Active Suspension Management (PASM) verfügt der Hochleistungssportwagen serienmäßig über ein weiteres aktives Regelsystem, das für optimale Fahrdynamik sorgt. Das rechnergesteuerte Dämpfungssystem profitiert von der Vernetzung mit PTM und PSM durch eine fahrdynamisch angepasste Regelung. Der Fahrer kann dabei zwischen Normal- und Sport-Modus wählen. Je nach Vorgabe reagiert die kontinuierliche Dämpferverstellung dabei entweder mehr komfortorientiert oder sportlich-straff. Das Fahrverhalten des neuen 911 Turbo passt sich so den ganz individuellen Wünschen des Fahrers an.

Die Porsche-Sicherheitsphilosophie verlangt, dass die Bremsleistung immer ein Mehrfaches über der Motorleistung liegt. So verzögern an der Vorderachse Sechskolben-Festsattelbremsen mit 350 Millimetern im Durchmesser messenden Bremsscheiben. Die gleich großen Scheiben an der Hinterachse werden von Vierkolben-Festsätteln in die Zange genommen. Wie für alle 911-Modelle steht auch für den neuen 911

Das optionale 19-Zoll Rad im RS Spyder-Design mit innovativem Zentralverschluss
Optional 19-inch wheels of RS Spyder design, with innovative central locking

In the new 911 Turbo, PTM communicates with Porsche Stability Management, which is also standard equipment. This high-performance sports car also has another active regulating system that ensures optimal road dynamics – Porsche Active Suspension Management (PASM). This is a computer-controlled damping system with dynamically regulated settings derived from PTM and PSM networking. Drivers can choose between Regular and Sport modes. Depending on this, the continuous shock absorber adjusting system is set to a more comfort-oriented setting or a firmer, sporty one. In other words, the new 911 Turbo's road behavior responds accurately to the driver's preferences.

Porsche's safety philosophy calls for brake system performance to be several times higher than the power the engine can develop. The six-piston fixed-caliper brakes at the front have 350 mm (13.8 in) diameter disks. Rear disks of the same diameter are gripped by four-piston fixed calipers. As for all 911 models, the Porsche Ceramic Composite Brake (PCCB) can be ordered as an option. This system, with 380 millimeter (15 inch) disks at the front,

Turbo die Porsche Ceramic Composite Brake (PCCB) zur Wahl. Die Keramikbremsanlage mit 380 Millimeter großen Bremsscheiben an der Vorderachse bietet noch schnelleres Ansprechverhalten, sehr hohe Fadingstabilität und absolute Korrosionssicherheit. Im Vergleich zur Serienbremsanlage mit Grauguss-Bremsscheiben wiegt die PCCB außerdem rund 18 Kilogramm weniger.

Ein charakteristisches Merkmal des stärksten Serien-Elfers ist die Bugverkleidung mit großen Kühlluft-öffnungen und den stegförmigen LED-Blinkern. Neu sind titanfarben lackierte Lamellen in den seitlichen Lufteinlässen und LED-Tagfahrleuchten an Stelle der bisherigen Nebelscheinwerfer. Das erstmals für den neuen 911 Turbo optional erhältliche dynamische Kurvenlicht verbessert durch sein bis zu 15 Grad in die Kurve schwenkendes Scheinwerfermodul die Ausleuchtung von Kurven im Straßenverlauf. Die anspruchsvolle Gestaltung des Doppellinsen-Projek-tionssystems transportiert den fortschrittlichen und markanten Charakter des neuen 911 Turbo in beson-derem Maße. Die neue Form der Doppelarm-Außen-spiegel bietet eine Vergrößerung der Sichtfläche nach

Leichtgewicht: Porsche Ceramic Composite Brake (PCCB)
Lightweight: the Porsche Ceramic Composite Brake (PCCB) system

responds even faster, is extremely resistant to fading and totally free from corrosion. Compared with the standard brake system, which has gray cast iron disks, PCCB cuts the car's weight by 18 kilograms (40 lbs).

A striking visual feature of the most powerful series-production Porsche 911 is the nose section of the body, with its large cooling air intakes and LED flasher strips. The titanium-color slats in the side air intakes are new, and so are the LED daytime driving lights that take the place of the previous fog lamps. Dynamic cornering light, a first-time option on the new 911 Turbo, uses headlamp units that can turn up to 15 degrees into a corner. The twin-lens projection system adds even more to the bold, progressive character of the new 911 Turbo. The double-arm outside mirrors are of a new pattern; they increase the rear-view area and their aerodynamic design reduces the amount of dirt reaching the mirror glass. For the new 911 Turbo, Porsche has developed forged 19-inch Turbo II wheels with a two-color finish for an unusually effective styling accent. Seen from the rear too, the new car conveys more massive strength

hinten und sorgt durch eine optimierte Aerodynamik für eine geringere Verschmutzung des Spiegelglases. Die für den neuen 911 Turbo entwickelten 19-Zoll Turbo II-Räder in Schmiedetechnik mit serienmäßiger Bi-Color-Optik setzen einen besonderen stilistischen Akzent. Beim neuen 911 Turbo ist die Heckansicht noch kraftvoller. Neben dem klassischen Spaltflügel sind dafür vor allem die neu gestalteten Rückleuchten in LED-Technik und die deutlich vergrößerten Endrohre verantwortlich.

In die jüngste Generation des Top-Elfers hat eine neue Lenkradgeneration Einzug gehalten. Bei Modellen mit Schaltgetriebe gehört ein neues Dreispeichen-Sportlenkrad mit geändertem Lenkraddesign zur Serienausrüstung. Für Fahrzeuge mit Porsche-Doppelkupplungsgetriebe steht erstmals als Alternative zum PDK-Lenkrad mit den bewährten Schiebetasten ein neues Dreispeichen-Sportlenkrad mit Schaltpaddles optional zur Verfügung. Diese Schaltpaddles sind lenkradfest montiert. Mit dem rechten wird hoch-, mit dem linken runtergeschaltet. In Verbindung mit dem optionalen »Sport Chrono Paket Turbo« verfügt sowohl das Paddle- als auch das PDK-Lenkrad mit Schiebetasten

Die geschmiedete Turbo-Felge in neuem Design
The forged Turbo wheels are of new design

RECHTE SEITE: Feinschliff im Design: Der neue 911 Turbo
RIGHT PAGE: *Subtle design refinements: the new 911 Turbo*

Das Dreispeichen-Sportlenkrad mit Schalt-Paddles
Three-spoke sport steering wheel with shift paddles

than ever before, due to the classic divided wing, but especially to the restyled rear lights using LED technology and the much larger exhaust tailpipes.

New-generation steering wheels are featured on the latest generation of the top 911 model. Cars with a manual-shift gearbox have a new three-spoke sport steering wheel of revised design as standard equipment. Customers who order the Porsche double-clutch transmission have an alternative for the first time: the PDK steering wheel with its much-appreciated sliding controls or a new sport three-spoke steering wheel with shift paddles fixed to it. The right paddle is used for upshifts, the left paddle for downshifts. If the optional "Sport Chrono Turbo" package is chosen, both the paddle steering wheel and the PDK version with its sliding controls are equipped with integral displays. Either "Sport" or "Sport Plus" lights up, depending on the function key that is pressed. If Launch Control is active, this is also shown. In cars with the standard PDK steering wheel, the displays are housed in an extra binnacle above the airbag module; if the new sport steering wheel with shift paddles is installed, they are in the right and left twin spokes.

über integrierte Anzeigen. In Abhängigkeit von der ge-
drückten Funktionstaste leuchtet die Anzeige »Sport«
beziehungsweise »Sport Plus«. Ist die Launch Control
aktiviert, wird dies ebenfalls dort angezeigt. Beim
serienmäßigen PDK-Lenkrad sind diese Anzeigen in
einer zusätzlichen Hutze oberhalb des Airbagmoduls
untergebracht, beim neuen Sportlenkrad mit Schalt-
paddles in der rechten und linken Doppelspeiche.

Der neue Porsche 911 Turbo verbindet tief greifende
technologische Neuerungen mit Feinschliff im Design.
In allen Kerneigenschaften wurde der Hochleistungssportwagen signifikant verbessert. Er ist sowohl
erheblich sparsamer und leichter als auch stärker,
schneller und noch dynamischer geworden. Die Zu-
kunft hat begonnen.

The new Porsche 911 Turbo high-performance sports
car combines fundamental technological innovations
with subtle design refinements, and has been
significantly improved in all its key properties. It is
now much lighter and more economical, but also more
powerful, faster and even more dynamic. The future
has begun!

Der ausfahrende
Heckspoiler verleiht der
typischen Turbo-Silhouette
noch mehr Dynamik
*More dynamic than ever:
the typical Turbo silhouette
with extending rear spoiler*

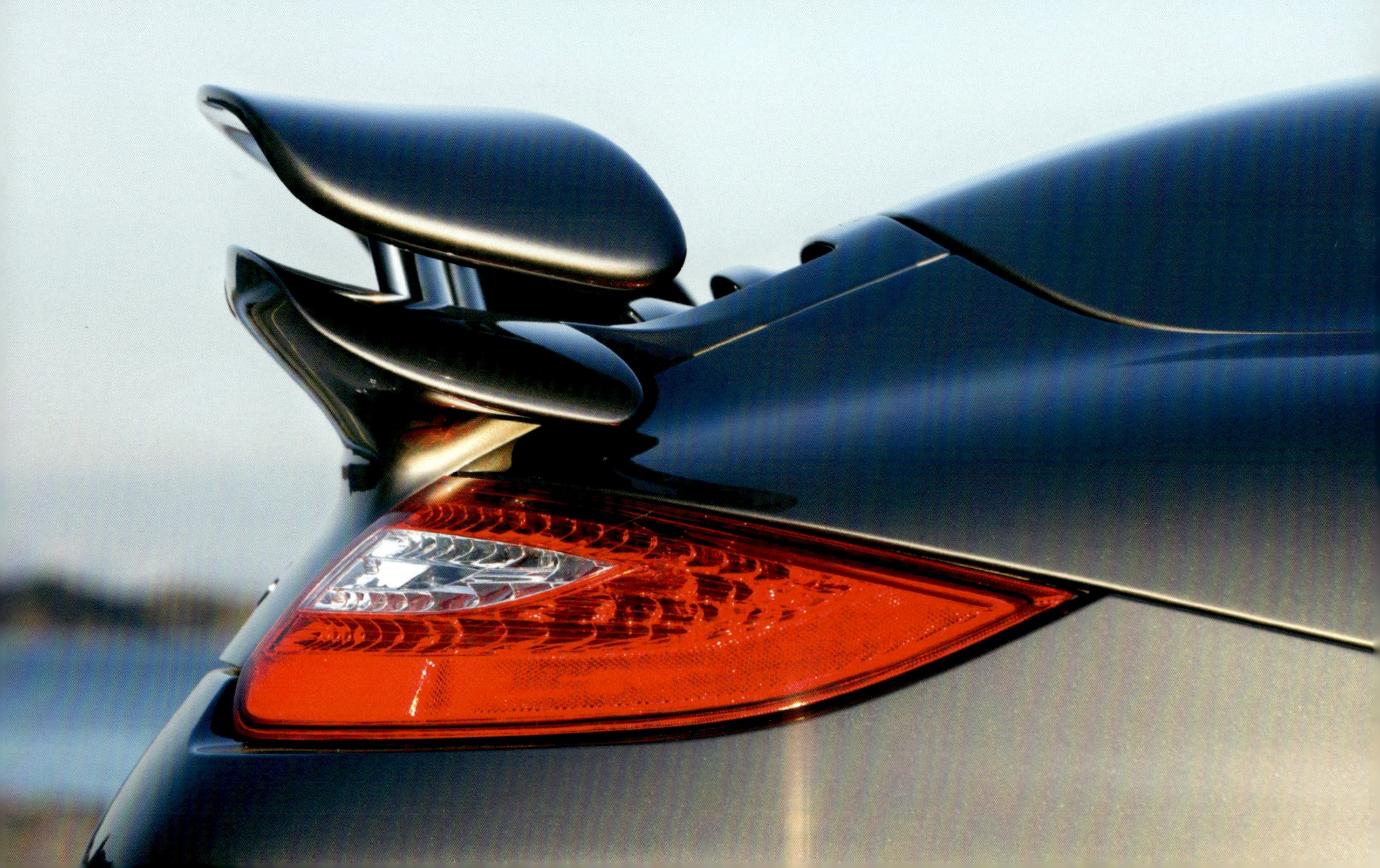

Dr. Ing. h. c. F. Porsche AG
Porscheplatz 1
70435 Stuttgart
Germany
www.porsche.com/museum

Inhalt & Abbildungen: Porsche AG, Historisches Archiv
Content & photos: Porsche AG, Historical Archives
Design & Layout: SEIDLDESIGN
Druck / Printing: GZD

© 2009 Edition Porsche-Museum, Stuttgart,
und DuMont Buchverlag, Köln

Erschienen im DuMont Buchverlag
www.dumont-buchverlag.de

ISBN 978-3-8321-9299-0
Printed in Germany